Praise for *Lead with*

Vicki Wilson's *Lead with Instructi*

for all educators because it is about organizational and leadership *intentionality,* which can increase teacher effectiveness and student achievement. Reflection and growth depend on such deliberate intentionality, and the team approach put forth here brings about trust and inclusion through a thoughtful, nonthreatening process. Classrooms that are ignored will never grow with any zest or zeal. Wilson fills a gap in the field with this brilliant, practical godsend of a book that can be implemented at your school starting right now.

—Rick Jetter, PhD, author of six books (including the highly acclaimed *Escaping the School Leader's Dunk Tank* and *Let Them Speak!*), keynote speaker, and cofounder of Pushing Boundaries

Enacting long-term change in a school is really hard. In *Lead with Instructional Rounds*, Vicki Wilson offers a process for teachers to observe each other teach, discuss best practices, reflect on school and personal goals, celebrate strengths, and set goals to continue their professional growth. Whether the school team is discussing effective practices in instruction, classroom culture, or effective behavior strategies, instructional rounds are a method for taking new learning and nurturing it to thrive inside your school, leading to lasting change.

—Brian Mendler, staff developer, podcaster, and author of nationally best-selling book *That One Kid* and new release *Watch Your Mouth*

In *Lead with Instructional Rounds*, veteran teacher, principal, and now author Vicki Wilson takes us down a path of personal growth and learning through instructional rounds, recognizing the power of observation, professional dialogue, and reflection among colleagues. Wilson weaves purpose, honest talk, transparency, and practical guidelines together to support you on your journey with instructional rounds. This playbook for a collaborative process is sure to create meaningful opportunities for more effective instruction and deeper learning for both staff and students.

—Jimmy Casas, educator, author, speaker, and leadership coach

Vicki Wilson has outlined a recipe for the most powerful opportunity for teachers to reflect on the impact of their own instructional practices. *Lead with Instructional Rounds* offers the what, why, and how to bring teachers within a building together to learn from one another in a safe and positive environment. Wilson shares her experience in preparing her teachers to maintain a system that thrives on positivity. The templates and examples will give readers a running start to bring instructional rounds to their own school. Wilson is committed to exposing what is working in her school and has shared the methods her staff has used to celebrate success and improve their individual and collective impact on student learning.

—Connie Hamilton, author of *Hacking Questions* and
curriculum director in Saranac Community Schools

Outside of school walls, it's no secret that the world is evolving at an accelerating pace. For what happens inside schools to remain relevant for the world our students and staff experience each day, building principals must lead the way. Simply put, instructional leadership is paramount to sustained change and a key to best-practice infusion. In *Lead with Instructional Rounds*, Vicki Wilson eloquently shares from her vast experiences and provides a blueprint for getting educators into each others classrooms to see the talents of colleagues, build trust, and take risks, all while being intentional and hyperfocused on high-quality instruction throughout the process.

—Thomas C. Murray, author of *Personal & Authentic: Designing Learning Experiences that Impact a Lifetime* and director of innovation for Future Ready Schools

Vicki Wilson has crafted a compelling book full of ready-to-use ideas to help schools get started with instructional rounds. Vicki helps readers understand the value of instructional rounds, as well as their unexpected benefits, and lays out a clear path for school leaders to follow. It's like couch-to-5K for instructional rounds with practical guidance for every step along the way. I highly recommend *Lead with Instructional Rounds* for administrators, teacher leaders, and staff book studies.

—Allyson Apsey, elementary principal and author of *Through the Lens of Serendipity*

Vicki's Wilson's *Lead with Instructional Rounds* is a fantastic read for both seasoned and aspiring leaders. Insights shared from her own personal journey are supportive, informative, and accessible, all qualities that describe who she is as a person. There are a number of books that address rounds as a process, but Vicki goes beyond the process and gets to the heart of the journey—and its purpose. If you are looking to implement instructional rounds in a transformative way, then you have just found the right book!

—Brian A. Peters, MEd, MSA, MBA, author, speaker, professor, and K–12 education consultant

In *Lead with Instructional Rounds*, Vicki Wilson shows both the rationale behind and the benefits of this practice as well as a step-by-step guide for implementation. She shares how instructional rounds help her team develop a common school language, provide opportunities for both horizontal and vertical observations, and promote collective efficacy for all. Most importantly, Vicki has developed a culture of trust and shared purpose through instructional rounds, which I have had the privilege of observing firsthand. This book is a must-read for any teacher, principal, or educational leader working to celebrate the best elements of each classroom and provide opportunities for growth from the expertise of the teacher next door!

—Jonathon Wennstrom, elementary principal,
Livonia Public Schools, Michigan

Lead with Instructional Rounds is a remarkable guide for educational leaders who want to drive positive change, support teacher growth, and improve daily classroom instruction. Vicki Wilson's transparency and thoughtful reflection will help you avoid the pitfalls that can come with executing a new initiative. The book provides a path for instructional staff to receive the feedback and encouragement they need to become their very best.

—Paul Liabenow, executive director, Michigan Elementary
and Middle School Principals Association

I strongly believe that everyone has a story that should be shared. Vicki Wilson not only has a story to share, she creates a movie in our head so we can see, feel, and hear the process of instructional rounds. After reading this playbook, any leader will have the tools to start the process in their own school. So many benefits of leading instructional rounds are shared by this authentic education leader.

—Syndee Malek, associate executive director and
leadership development consultant, MEMSPA

Lead with Instructional Rounds

A LEAD Like a PIRATE Guide

LEAD With Instructional Rounds

Creating a Culture of Professional Learning

Vicki Wilson

Lead with Instructional Rounds: Creating a Culture of Professional Learning

Published by Dave Burgess Consulting, Inc.
San Diego, CA
DaveBurgessConsulting.com

Cover and Interior Design by Liz Schreiter

Library of Congress Control Number: 2020932553
Paperback ISBN: 978-1-951600-12-9
E-book ISBN: 978-1-951600-13-6

DEDICATION

To all the teachers I currently work with and have worked with at Monroe Elementary School. I am honored to walk through the halls with you every day as we grow and learn together. Thank you for taking risks, working harder than any staff I know, and allowing me to lead this fine school. You fill my heart with pride every day! XO

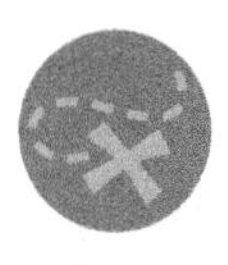

CONTENTS

FOREWORD

Shelley Burgess and Beth Houf

Beth and I (and many of you) know that being a school or district administrator can be lonely at times. When we decided to write *Lead Like a PIRATE*, it was with the intent to help support other educators by sharing our stories and the strategies that have worked for us as educational leaders. We wanted to be sure that no one felt as if they were alone in this important work. Our goal was, and continues to be, to work together to set up systems of support through our professional learning network (PLN) and to empower leaders to take risks to ensure that school is an amazing place for both students and staff.

Since the book's release, it has been inspiring to watch our #LeadLAP crew grow. The examples and stories shared daily with the hashtag are so inspiring. What we have come to realize is that we are surrounded by greatness that needs a voice. One evening after our book was published, we started brainstorming how we could continue to support leaders in a new way. One thing that stood out to us is how easy it is for leaders to get overwhelmed by the sheer volume of information being shared at what seems like lightning speed. There is so much we either need or want to learn. So we chatted about ways we might offer bite-sized expertise for leaders so they can make an even bigger impact on their schools, and the Lead Like a PIRATE guides were born.

We are thrilled to have Vicki Wilson author our sixth Lead Like a PIRATE guide, *Lead with Instructional Rounds.* Anyone who follows #LeadLAP knows that the mantra at its core is culture first, culture next, culture always. What Vicki has done with instructional rounds has dramatically transformed the culture at her school, and with this book that transformation will spread to cultures at many more schools. To us, instructional rounds are a lot like professional learning communities in the sense that just about every educational leader has heard of them and many claim to be using them in their schools, but not everyone is implementing them at the deep level that creates significant positive change.

In *Lead with Instructional Rounds,* Vicki shares her story of having to merge two schools into one and the resulting need to change the toxic culture that resulted from the merge into a thriving one where students and teachers learn at high levels. Her school is literally one where students and teachers are running to get *in*, rather than *out*.

As we share in *Lead Like a PIRATE,* the work we do as leaders to support all of our teachers in improving their craft is one of the most impactful things we do. Our potential to do what's best for kids often lies in our ability to inspire, influence, and support the adults in our educational system. Vicki does this brilliantly through the use of instructional rounds.

In *Lead with Instructional Rounds,* Vicki throws the doors of her school wide open and shares her work. She leaves nothing out. In addition to sharing all of the successes and the benefits, she shares the research she's done, the struggles she's faced, and the obstacles she's overcome. She walks you step by step through the journey she has taken over the years with her team and provides you with a guide for how you, too, can do this work in YOUR school. If you are looking for a way to dramatically improve student learning, transform your school culture into one of positive collaborative learning, and create a system to support the self-reflection and professional growth of your teachers, look no further than *Lead with Instructional Rounds.* We enthusiastically encourage you to read this book, connect with Vicki, and take the first step on your journey to #LeadWithRounds.

INTRODUCTION

Like so many teachers, I spent each August eagerly preparing my classroom, determining my classroom management plan, and writing my first weeks of lessons. During these busy and exciting days, I relished my professional and personal chats with colleagues about new textbooks, new district initiatives, summer adventures, and such. Then the new year began, and I welcomed my new class of fourth graders and closed the door. Like the majority of American teachers, I expected to spend my time in the classroom alone with the students, no chatting with colleagues—for reasons personal or professional.

Schools are (and have always been) structured for the isolation of teachers. It is like we are our own little silos. While there was another teacher and another class on each side of me and yet another teacher and another class across the hall, none of us had any idea what the others did.

In my twenties, I worked across the hall from my best friend, Cindy. We both taught fourth grade at James Rodgers Elementary School in St. Clair Shores, Michigan. We ate lunch together every day. We socialized after school and on weekends. I knew pretty much everything about Cindy, and she knew pretty much everything about me. I would borrow supplies from her; I would sit in her classroom and chat; I even hid a fart machine in her room and used my remote from the hallway to set it off (repeatedly). *Yet I never saw Cindy teach.* I completely missed the opportunity to watch her do the most important thing in the world—teach children. Maybe she had a special gift of connecting with kids, while across the hallway I was trying desperately to engage a student who was completely withdrawn from learning and was avoiding social interactions with peers. Perhaps Cindy was trying to find an instructional strategy that increased student collaboration and innovation and would have appreciated seeing the way I prompted students to create a live storyboard to demonstrate their understanding of the challenges that enslaved persons faced in attempting to flee for freedom.

Spending years of your career (or your entire career) in isolation is nothing but a massive amount of missed opportunities for teachers and students. Isn't it crazy that in the business of learning, growth, and development, we actually operate in a way that impedes *adult* learning, growth, and development? Think for a moment about the profound negative impact that has on students.

How can we grow when the professional work we do is done alone? In my fourteen years as a teacher, the only time I saw one of my colleagues teach was when I would step into their classroom on my prep to borrow something (or to get my fart machine back). And then, I wasn't observing the art of that educator's instructional choices or decisions; I was actually interrupting the teacher and the class.

As schools are structured for isolated work, it is imperative we put systems for collaboration in place that overcome the obstacles of teacher seclusion. Professional learning communities (PLCs) have been a gift to education because they set up norms and protocols for teacher collaboration in planning, evaluating learning, and responding to the results. Teachers working in a PLC can talk about what they are teaching, how the students are learning, and the strategies they used to get the results they shared. This is a great model for teacher development that is founded upon the collaborative work of teachers and professional dialogue for the purpose of improving learning for all of our students.

What if we added a school-wide system for not only discussing our instructional practices but actually observing members of our PLC executing these strategies with their students while we engage in self-reflection of our own teaching practices? What if we also observed teachers in other grade levels to help us see the vertical interdependence of each grade level within the school? We could see how we all contribute our own pieces to the full puzzle of preparing students to become contributing members of society.

This is where instructional rounds come in. I taught for fourteen years before becoming a principal. Within the first month of my first year as a principal, I quickly realized the need to bring teachers into their colleagues' classrooms. The problem was that I didn't know how to do it logistically, and I wasn't sure how to create the culture that would not only accept it but embrace it.

Instructional rounds are a process for educators, in small collaborative groups, to observe their colleagues teaching while reflecting on their own practices, followed by dialogue about effective instruction and the impact on learning. The group follows a simple protocol of observing their colleagues teach, noticing the impact their colleagues' methods have on student learning, and immediately debriefing to discuss best practices of instruction and learning with each other. Throughout the process, the observers engage in reflective thought about their own instructional practices and consider how they can grow and improve in their work with their own students. When a school engages in ongoing and frequent instructional rounds, the teachers in that school develop a shared understanding of best instructional practices, develop improved pedagogical skills, collaborate regularly, and grow professionally—as individual educators and as a school team.

In its 2017 report and research brief *Effective Teacher Professional Development*, the Learning Policy Institute identified seven key features of effective professional development. In its study, the institute reviewed three decades of literature on structured professional learning that resulted in changes in teacher practices and improvements in student learning. Their findings stated that effective professional development incorporates most, if not all, of the following elements:

- It is content focused.
- It incorporates active learning.
- It supports collaboration in job-embedded contexts.
- It uses models and modeling of effective practice.
- It provides coaching and expert support.
- It offers opportunities for feedback and reflection.
- It is of sustained duration.

When I implemented instructional rounds at Monroe Elementary, I found all seven elements already ingrained in the process. To begin with, instructional rounds are a job-embedded process that engages the participants in active and interactive learning within the classrooms of their own school. Each observing teacher enters a classroom and examines a peer (modeling instruction) while they enter into reflective thought about their own practices and classroom. During the observation, the facilitator plans debriefing questions intended to engage the group in collaborative dialogue on effective practices as they relate to the content of the lesson. For example, after observing a reading lesson, the group will discuss best practices of literacy instruction. The debriefing conversation is interactive, reflective, and offers feedback to each speaker's thoughts and ideas and often includes coaching by the facilitator or another member of the group with expertise on the topic being discussed. The process ends with each observer giving written positive feedback to each teacher they observed during that round. Instructional rounds are intended to be a sustained and regularly scheduled practice for educators in a school. Schools may schedule rounds each semester, quarterly, or monthly.

Robert Marzano writes, "Instructional rounds are one of the most valuable tools that a school or district can use to enhance teachers' pedagogical skills and develop a culture of collaboration." Instructional rounds allow for thoughtful and deliberate reflective questioning that both validates best practices being executed in a school and leads to supportive conversations as we challenge ourselves to grow and improve individually and collectively. Through these practices, we can create a school-wide culture of collaboration and professional learning.

Instructional rounds are a school practice in which the leader promotes and participates as a leader, a learner, or both. A 2008 meta-analysis to study the impact of leadership on student outcomes found that leaders who promote and participate in teacher learning and development yield an effect size of 0.84 on student outcomes. (Effect size is a measurement often used by educational researchers to determine the effectiveness of a particular intervention, to compare different interventions, or to evaluate student growth over time.) This result applies to both formal and informal contexts, and the study describes "promoting and participating" as being more involved than just supporting or sponsoring staff development. To put this 0.84 effect size into perspective, consider that a 0.4 effect size indicates a moderate impact on student learning and is considered the hinge point for the effect a practice or innovation has for positive change on student achievement. In other words, a practice that has a 0.4 effect size or greater is a worthwhile implementation for increasing student achievement and is deemed by John Hattie as the "zone of desired effects." An effect size of 0.6 has a large impact on achievement. So an effect size of 0.84 is significant.

Just like high-performing professional learning communities, instructional rounds will only be effective if they are established in a school culture of trust and vulnerability. Five years after becoming a principal, after reading the work of the experts in the field and going through very hard times and challenges as a school leader, I finally began to develop a method for instructional rounds that thrives in a place of trust and vulnerability.

At the elementary school where I am the principal, our journey of growth and learning through instructional rounds has led us to develop a school-wide system that engages teachers in conscious self-reflection. Our instructional rounds process allows teachers a moment each month to pause within the chaos of their day to engage in intentional observation of other teachers and reflect on their own instructional practices and the impact they have on their students. This ongoing practice of instructional rounds is the most valuable professional-development experience our teachers engage in at our school.

The purpose of this book is to share our journey and work as well as give you an easy-to-implement playbook for conducting instructional rounds in your school. My hope is that you can take this approach and implement it in your school to support the self-reflection and professional growth of teachers and build a school culture of positive collaborative learning.

Thank you for taking the time to read this book, and more importantly, thank you for being an educator. I hope that through these pages you will learn a process that will cause transformational growth of educators and improve school-wide practices in your school.

Lead with Instructional Rounds

SO THIS IS WHAT "PRINCIPAL-ING" IS?

After teaching for fourteen years in two districts and three different schools, I was given the exciting opportunity to be an elementary school principal—a leader of adult learners and of instruction. I remember two unexpected lessons sticking out to me the most in my first few months as a building principal.

September was approaching, and I was eagerly anticipating and planning the beginning of the school year and the first day that I was to report to work as the principal of McKinley Elementary School in Wyandotte, Michigan. I was strong and ready on the outside, but inside I was worried that I wouldn't know what to do in this new role. *What if I am terrible at being a principal? What if I don't know the answers? I don't even know what the questions will be!* I was also a relatively new mom—my daughter Mia was one and a half years old. This new role was different from teaching kids, and teaching was my professional passion. I was really good at teaching (at least that is what people told me).

I went in that first day determined that I was not going to make up answers but that I would present myself with the very best fake confidence I could possibly muster.

Within twenty minutes on my first day on the job, Jo, the daytime facility and maintenance employee, approached me with a distressing situation regarding the pear tree on the backside of school property. She shared that the tree had been planted by a class, and it was a sacred marker for the school. Then she said it was slated to be cut and removed within the next few days by the district. She said this tree was special for the school and that I needed to stop this action.

"OK, how do I stop this?" I was sure I was not going to have a voice because this decision had already been made by the district.

Jo looked at me strangely and said, "You are the principal, and this is your school." She was probably just as puzzled as I was—but for different reasons. Jo was operating under the assumption that in the formal organizational system my new title and rank carried enough influence for me to simply reverse this decision. I was a naïve first-day principal. I believed my influence was the same as it was the day before. I had absolutely no expertise on trees; therefore, I should not have any control over the fate of a tree located on the school's property.

She told me to call the director of operations and simply tell him he could not cut down the tree because it was *special*. Now, I had worked as a teacher at this school for three years before becoming the principal, and I had no idea the tree was special. I like trees, but I didn't really notice or know anything about this tree. So I took Jo's word that its specialness dated from before my time and I was just unaware of it.

Taking Jo's advice, I called the director of operations. Once I had him on the phone, I told him what Jo told me. "Ed, the tree that is intended to be removed is very special. I don't think it should be removed."

His reply was very short and very clear. "OK. We will leave it there. You are the principal."

I suppose some would have liked this response and loved this newfound power, but I must admit that it put me in a place of great discomfort. *How can my new title influence an action such as this?* I didn't even give a good reason (frankly, I didn't have one). For fourteen years as a teacher I had acted with purpose and sought out support from my administration for any change initiative by sharing a specific purpose and the positive impact it would have on students. That day I made a phone call based on one person's opinion that I didn't have full understanding of, and that phone call led to a quick decision that lacked justification. If it had been two months earlier when I was still a fourth-grade teacher, no one would have listened to me about that tree.

That first day as a principal was when I first understood the concept of a position of power. I honestly didn't like it. *Now what? What if I make a mistake? From this day forward, every mistake I make will be bigger and worse than my mistakes were as a teacher! I was a really good teacher (I think), but what if I fail as a principal?!*

Ironically, one year later that special pear tree was struck by lightning and had to be cut down. Hmmm. Undoubtedly, there was a deep lesson there. I am not sure what it was exactly, but I will tell you, I felt that in some way the world righted itself that day from my mistake. For the record, saving a tree was not the mistake—my naïve leadership decisions were.

Today, as a leader and principal, I work each day to always act with purpose. If our students and teachers have no purpose or opportunity for growth, there is no reason to invest time and effort in the school day. But instructional rounds can help to clarify and spark that sense of purpose and provide opportunity for that growth. The effects they've had on both adult and student learning is incredible.

• • • •

You know that intense, innocent zeal you feel your first year of teaching? I think it is the same for your first year as a principal. I viewed myself as an instructional leader, and I could not wait to get into classrooms and work with teachers. I was the brand-new principal of the school I had been a teacher at for the three years prior. It was perfect (in my head) because I had not been there too long, yet I had been there long enough to have relationships. I knew the needs and strengths of the school and the staff. I had a sense of our growth opportunities. Just like every year I had taught, I had a driving mission to make a difference. Now I would make a difference as a principal. Now I would make a difference beyond the walls of my fourth-grade classroom. I was going to make a difference in the whole school.

My first mission was the work I was most excited about—improving teaching and learning. I needed to get in classrooms to observe and then talk to teachers. I prepared a lot on how to give feedback; I studied educational research on the best instructional practices; and I wanted to make teachers better. It started out very well. I felt like I was living my dream! It was easy and fun. My teachers loved the feedback, and we all played nice. I was growing the team while building a happy culture and remaining safe by interacting with my team in the friendliest kind of way. I wasn't taking risks—yet. I was not pushing my staff outside of their comfort zones.

Going into the classrooms of the colleagues I used to teach with was beyond eye-opening. As a teacher in isolation, I am not proud to say that I made judgments about my peers while I taught with them. Without ever seeing them teach, I had an opinion about who was a "good" teacher and who was not. Finally, as a principal, I went into everyone's room often. Some of my previously held judgments were honestly unfair—one way or another. My assumptions didn't match my observations. Either way, I was hit hard by the amount of work I found to be done. As an educator, I did not know or appreciate my colleagues' strengths. As a principal, I saw that *every* teacher had strengths and growth opportunities that I was completely unaware of when I was their teaching colleague. My teachers were just as differentiated as my fourth-grade students were.

I have found that educators don't share their observations on other teachers' strengths and growth opportunities. In fact, they may not even be aware of their own strengths or areas in need of improvement. I had much learning to do as a leader. I asked myself, "How do I help our teachers to see what their colleagues are doing in *their* classrooms so that they can reflect on their own practices and learn from the strengths of each other?" I asked myself that question in year one. I then wrestled with that question for the next five years.

Remember how I mentioned that I had my (risk-free) dream job? That didn't last. In the beginning of my second year as a principal I gave birth to twin boys, Matthew and Zachary. I returned from maternity leave excited and ready to move forward with the work of helping teachers grow while this concept of getting teachers in each other's rooms to learn from each other was still percolating in my head. Within a month of returning from my maternity leave, my superintendent, Pat, came for an unexpected visit. Pat shared that a decision would be made within the next couple of weeks to close our school. Financially, the district would not be able to absorb the cost of our declining enrollment, and our school would close at the end of that year. She advised me to establish transition teams to lay out the details of the merge.

I took a very deep breath and said, "OK." I tried to hold back the tears, knowing I was about to face my first incredibly challenging task as an inexperienced school leader. After Pat left, I gathered my composure and went to my computer to Google "transition team." I had no idea what I was doing. Things got real hard, real fast. The next three years were some of the hardest in my career; those years also taught me much about being a leader. I was still the principal at my new school, and our first instructional rounds eventually happened . . . five years later. Much of the framework we developed and continue to use today was the result of those challenging lessons we learned closing a school and then merging with another.

Grown-Up Lessons

Inevitably, the decision was made to close McKinley Elementary School. The district plan was to merge the entire student body of McKinley with the neighboring elementary school of Monroe Elementary in Wyandotte, Michigan. The current principal of Monroe was going to retire, which would create a place for me as the new leader of the two newly merged schools. I quickly learned that these two schools were polar opposites in their culture and day-to-day functions. It was like a divorce, a death, and the creation of a new blended family all in one thirty-second span. McKinley's home was being taken away, and all the children, many teachers, and "mom" were moving in with the new family. Monroe was losing their "dad" (retiring principal, Mr. Strait), and a new unknown "mom" was moving in to take over, bringing her beloved family. McKinley lost their home, and Monroe lost their parent. Both schools lost their identity.

How do you establish trust in this scenario? Two schools, polar opposites, neither wanting to lose their identity. We were the McKinley Tigers, and they were the Monroe Pandas. The problem was that each identity was unique enough to prevent a compromise. Seeing no compromise, I needed to learn what the sacred traditions of each school were so that they could be honored while building a new shared vision to create new traditions both schools could honor. McKinley valued their peace pole. It was a stone structure with the word *peace* written on it in several languages. The peace pole was moved to the new school property. Monroe valued their panda mural, and a promise was made that it would remain in place. These representations, while seemingly superficial, were important in that difficult transition, and honoring them, at that time, helped everyone move forward. Trust developed slowly and over time. One thing we learned was that having trust and feeling safe with each other was important to us, and it became critical to the success of our instructional rounds.

It was clear during the first year after the merge that the school had two different factions and a neutral group. The children were the first to show us all the path, of course. They appreciated their new friends. The staff came together next. Using the school improvement plan, we established what was nonnegotiable to keep all staff members on the same page. The parent group was the hardest challenge. It was hard for them to embrace a new school or a new vision. I suppose when you bring your child to school for the first day of kindergarten you do not envision school closures, mergers, and challenges.

I remember vividly the sixth year after the merge. That was the year students who had been part of our newly merged school since they were in kindergarten moved on from fifth grade to the middle school. It was very healing. We learned that teamwork and unity are better than factions and isolation. Those ideals are now a strong premise of our instructional rounds.

Dealing with sabotage was the most difficult lesson. I suppose that under the circumstances the reasoning and hurt behind sabotage can be understood. Sabotage happened in both expected ways as well as unexpected ways in the first few years. Our newly formed stepfamily had much work to do. In addition to reinventing ourselves, I could see that our school-wide instructional practices needed much improvement. Not everyone agreed we needed to improve or change, so I spent a lot of time sharing educational research and leading learning activities with our teachers. For the first time as a leader, I started to intentionally push my educators into a place of disruption. Beliefs and past practices were challenged. I was not always as liked as I had been when I was a teacher, which was often lonely for me. I distinctly remember when a group of parents from Monroe went to a school board meeting to publicly criticize my administrative decision to restructure our reading and writing instruction and a McKinley teacher who supported me. Their statements were harsh and sounded informed by discussions we had as a staff, which led to suspicion among staff members. This triggered greater division between the two teacher groups. At the end of that year, many teachers chose to transfer out of our school, and we had to again adjust and continue our work.

The next year we continued to grow, and I continued to push and hold high expectations for pursuing research-based best practices in the instructional work we did at our school. I was happy to see that through this intentional disruption of our beliefs and practices my teaching staff was beginning to unite. However, I realized many were uniting for the common cause of pushing back against me. We trudged through two years of private meetings and union consultations. I put curtains on my office windows so that I could close them and cry without anyone seeing. It was a difficult time for our school, and more teachers transferred out. By holding tight to a strong mission and vision and standing firm on decisions made that were best for our students, we eventually came out of that storm as better educators than when we entered.

I didn't know it at that time as a young principal, but that was my first experience leading second-order change. It was unbelievably hard. Later in my career I learned the difference between first-order change and second-order change, and then it made sense. First-order change is simply a change within an existing system, such as relocating from one classroom to another or adjusting to new start and end times in your school day. Second-order change is much more difficult to navigate through and incredibly difficult to lead. Second-order change challenges one's beliefs and alters the system as we know it. Whether a person makes the decision to change or is being forced to change, a second-order change requires new learning and is often uncomfortable. Changing the design of your instruction from traditional whole-group direct teaching to a differentiated small-group approach embedding a high degree of student choice and voice is likely to be a second-order change for most educators.

As we emerged from this time of transformation and growth, I realized we started to find our new school identity. Monroe Elementary School was a learning institution dedicated to both student learning and adult learning. We also identified as an organization that makes decisions based on educational research and best practices. It was good, and I was proud. I still respect my colleagues who decided to leave during those turbulent years.

Our new school learned how to grow from internal interference but not without learning major lessons. Through these lessons, we learned that positivity and transparency are necessary for our instructional rounds' success.

Our school culture was growing into its new identity of being a learning-focused school that valued adult learning just as much as student learning. Reading and engaging in educational dialogue were a normal part of our professional work. Yet, after learning and talking, teachers would go into the isolation of their own classrooms and apply their new knowledge in their own way. That was it. If it worked, great. If it didn't go as planned, oh well. Perhaps each teacher personally reflected on how well a new strategy worked and then chose to continue the practice, abandon it, or adjust it. A practice may have worked amazingly well for one second-grade teacher, and the same strategy may have totally flopped for a colleague.

We never really knew what happened in our classrooms after our adult learning and professional development. To truly grow as educators, we realized our need for personal reflection as well as collaborative and school-wide reflection. Instructional rounds became the system we used to regularly engage in personal, collaborative, and school-wide reflection.

The Catalyst

They say it takes three to five years to create a culture. Four years after our two schools merged, we finally had our first instructional round. At this point, our culture was healing well from the closure of one school, the merger, and the challenges of second-order change. I believed that instructional rounds, if done with the right purpose and intention, would continue to heal our staff and bring greater unity. I read and studied the research on instructional rounds and classroom walk-throughs. I planted the seeds with the staff for at least one year prior to our first round. Honestly, I was the hold up. It was me. I was ready to execute it (professionally); I was informed on how to do it, but I didn't take the plunge. I even had plenty of staff on board, and still I didn't launch the plan. Looking back, I wonder what my hesitation was. Was it fear of failure? After all, I had been working this through in my head for quite some time. We were in year four of our merged school, and we were getting along. The instructional shifts we made were finally embraced by the staff, and there was very little resistance. What if launching something new brought back the turbulent waters we had just navigated out of? I was healing too. What if it didn't go well? Was I ready for something I was so passionate about to potentially fail? I believed this would be good for my teachers and our school. I believed they would grow professionally and gain greater respect by watching each other teach. That is, if we had enough trust to open our doors and let people in. Were we there yet? Had we healed enough to have trust in the process and each other? My hope was that we were ready. My fear was that we were not. I never actually made the decision to launch the first iteration of instructional rounds at my school—my staff did. And for that I am forever grateful!

One winter, a group of teachers formed a study group around the idea of a Math Workshop. Though they were gathering every other week to have a dialogue about what they were doing in their own classrooms, they felt that seeing it in action would help them grow. They asked me if I could find a way for them to get into one another's (isolated) classrooms to see how they were trying to implement the Math Workshop. That was when I saw the opportunity. I refer to this as the "catalyst" in our instructional rounds journey. I agreed to set the observations up and shared that I wanted to do them in an instructional rounds style—meaning that we would visit each room for a short time. The observing group would then exit the room to debrief and continue that protocol until we visited all the rooms involved. We would then conclude with a team discussion about the big ideas from our observations. Since our staff meetings were on Wednesday afternoons, I strategically set this first attempt at instructional rounds on a Wednesday so that we could end the day by sharing this experience with the whole staff—that is, if it went well. I had an entire plan B staff meeting agenda prepared just in case it was a disaster.

On a Wednesday morning, we observed half of the teachers who wanted to participate in this experiment. After each visit we stepped into the hallway to talk about the Math Workshop practices in place and the impact on student learning. In the afternoon we switched—the hosts became the observers, and the observers became the hosts. We continued to debrief after each observation and concluded with a whole-group discussion with reflection and ideas for personal improvement. Not only did the process go well but there was an air of excitement and an eagerness from the teachers to immediately implement the new ideas and strategies that grew out of their observations and personal reflections.

At the end of the day, we gathered as a whole group for our staff meeting. The plan B agenda was thrown out, and we spent the entire meeting talking about the experiences of the day and the concept of improving our practices using the process of instructional rounds. It was wonderfully contagious! The rest of the staff asked questions about the process and how we could continue working in this style. We brainstormed what we needed as a staff in order to fully commit to using this approach in developing ourselves. The ideals we needed came from our lessons learned during our first years together. Those ideals included establishing trust, feeling safe, building unity, emphasizing positivity, and ensuring transparency. At the close of this meeting, we decided that we would develop a system for professional growth using instructional rounds. But first we needed to clarify why and how we would do instructional rounds and what areas we would use them for. In other words, we needed to set parameters and develop a playbook.

OUR INSTRUCTIONAL ROUNDS PLAYBOOK

The single greatest influence on the professional practice of teachers is the direct observation of other teachers.

—DOUGLAS B. REEVES

The story of instructional rounds brings together the "feeling" brain and the "thinking" brain for the purpose of improving teaching and learning and strengthening school culture. Setting up instructional rounds needs to satisfy both parts of the brain for all educators involved. The initial meeting should clearly establish the agreements you have decided are important to the staff. This is their safety net. The emotional brain needs this meeting and the critical agreements so it can trust the process and allow the thinking brain to take risks. The emotional brain is always on the lookout for threats. By putting guidelines and boundaries in place, the threat is reduced or eliminated.

Premise and Definition

Before we began school-wide instructional rounds, we put the following statement in writing. This became our premise:

> "The answer is in the room" is our approach to professional development. Our most effective means of staff development does not come from listening to "experts" discuss what has worked within schools or districts with a different fingerprint and/or philosophy. Instead, our most effective learning can take place by observing one another and having reflective conversations about what works well with students at Monroe Elementary School.

Then we began to attempt a definition. Remembering our need for transparency as a school that recently struggled with trust and factions, the easiest way we found to define instructional rounds for our school was to write two specific lists. First, our staff came up with a list detailing what the instructional rounds process is.

- It is an opportunity to watch other teachers teach and see how children learn.
- It is an opportunity to observe quality teaching techniques and see the impact these techniques have on real students and their learning.
- It is a process designed to encourage self-reflection about your teaching and reflection about student learning.

- It is intended to encourage and enhance reflective dialogue among teachers regarding quality teaching and learning.
- It is an opportunity to reflect with colleagues about the positive things that other staff do to encourage student engagement, ensure students are learning, and improve teaching and learning in all classrooms.

Then our staff came up with a list detailing what the instructional rounds process is *not*.

- It is not used as part of the teacher evaluation process.
- It is not mandatory for staff to participate.
- It is not an opportunity to reflect with colleagues on the negative aspects of another teacher's classroom environment or methodologies.

Guide for Teachers

At the beginning of each school year, we send the following guide for instructional rounds to all staff:

Q: What should I expect on the day of instructional rounds if my classroom is being observed?

- Approximately four or five staff members will quietly enter your classroom to observe. If the children are active, we may mingle with the students and ask specific questions about their current task and learning. No seating is necessary for any of the adults involved in the observation.
- We have no expectation that you will stop what you are doing to acknowledge us or dialogue with us. Feel free to continue as if we were not in your classroom.
- We will only be staying in your classroom for approximately ten minutes. Once we leave, we will have a short conversation in the hallway about the positive instructional practices and their impact on student learning we observed in your classroom. This is a positive experience, and our comments will be about only the positive things we observed.
- Relax and have fun.

Q: What should I expect on the day of instructional rounds if I am observing other classrooms?

- Please meet in the PLC room at the beginning of the observation session.
- After a brief discussion about the process and commitments, we will begin visiting four classrooms. We'll stay approximately ten minutes in each room.
- Following each classroom visit, we will discuss the positive aspects of teaching and learning observed in that classroom with one another in the hallway before observing in the next classroom.
- Please drop a short email or note to the teachers you observed, with positive feedback and reactions to what you observed in the classroom.
- The observation process should take approximately fifteen minutes per classroom (eighty to ninety minutes total) including travel time between classes.
- You will summarize your insights and learning after the observations by sharing your responses to two additional reflective questions before returning back to your classroom.
- Relax and have fun.

Q: Who should I contact if I have other questions about the process?

- You can speak with the building principal or any teacher who has already participated in this activity.

Instructional Rounds in Practice

During instructional rounds, a small group of teachers (usually three to five) visit four of their colleagues' classrooms in the school. An instructional leader, typically the school principal, facilitates the process by establishing the norms in a preround meeting and reviewing the schedule. An instructional coach or teacher leader may also facilitate the process. The facilitator should have strong instructional knowledge; know the strengths of the host teachers; and know the strengths, needs, and growth opportunities of the observing teachers. It is also beneficial for the leader to know the inner workings of the school system: professional expectations, current goals, professional-development priorities, and growth opportunities of the school as a whole.

The Premeeting

When I have shared instructional rounds with other educators, I have taken a moment to ask my teachers what they feel is the most important thing I needed to share with others. Every teacher has told me that, by far, the most important part is the premeeting message. They have even stated that if I were to skip it, even once, they would likely feel uncomfortable beginning the visitations.

It is through this premeeting message that the objective of creating a safe space is met. Every safety net the teachers need is verbalized in the premeeting. The observing teachers and the facilitator are present for the premeeting. It sounds something like this:

> Welcome, everyone. We are here today for the purpose of instructional rounds. Instructional rounds are a positive, effective, and practical professional development experience. This collegial experience is intended to be a safe way we can support and grow

each other in this profession. It is an opportunity for us, as the observing teachers, to reflect on our own practices as we observe our colleagues teaching so that we can improve and grow as instructors.

Before visiting classrooms, I would like to review our professional agreements when participating in rounds. First, we all professionally agree that we will only speak of the positives in any and all post-communication. We are all aware students will have imperfect moments. We know teachers have imperfect moments too. We all know it happens, and if it happens during one of our visits, we will not discuss it with anyone. We will not discuss it while we debrief, we will not talk about it in the staff room, and we will not talk about it in the parking lot. We will honor our human right to make mistakes by understanding and letting them go.

Please make it comfortable for the students and teacher of the classrooms we visit. Try to get into the room and sit down with kids or find an open space at a table so that it feels natural for the class and the host teacher. When we are in the classroom, please speak quietly if you engage with each other or with the students.

We have an agreement that we will each drop a positive note or email to each teacher we visit today. This is the host teachers' only form of feedback and is a means for expressing our gratitude to each of our hosts today. It is most appreciated when you write specific insights, excitements, or takeaways from what

> happened in their class that will help you to grow and improve as a teacher.
>
> Please take pictures in the classroom for your professional use. I also encourage you to take pictures to tweet out. Please share your learning in the tweet, and include our school hashtag and #LeadWithRounds.
>
> I will monitor time. When you see me step into the hallway, please follow me. We will circle up right outside the classroom door to think and talk about the actions we observed that had a positive impact on student learning.

Highlighting the positives and individual strengths of all members of your staff feels wonderful to their emotional brain. This allows their thinking brain to feel safe and to dive into a self-reflective mode, comparing the work of their colleagues to their own work. Their thinking brain then evaluates their own application of instructional practices while contemplating how to improve in the work they do with their own students. Once again, this will not fully happen if there is any perceived threat by their emotional brain. This is a critical reason why instructional rounds can never be tied to teacher evaluation.

I have been in classrooms for rounds before and have noticed something that I would have otherwise posed as a question to the teacher and perhaps engaged in a coaching opportunity. For rounds, that line can never be crossed. I let it go. And I am completely okay with letting it go because the professional growth a teacher receives through instructional rounds is far greater than any teacher-evaluation protocol or supervisor-employee conversation. Best practice tells us homework should be risk-free practice and not graded. I stand firm on the principle that instructional rounds should also be risk-free development and never evaluated.

The Facilitator

After the norms have been set in the preround meeting, the facilitator shares the schedule of the day, and the group visits the four classrooms on their schedule. In each classroom, the group spends ten minutes observing the teaching and learning and then steps out into the hallway to debrief for five minutes following the observation. During the debriefing, the facilitator poses reflective questions to guide the positive conversation. This process is repeated in each of the four classrooms the group visits.

It is important that the facilitator watches the time. Each classroom teacher hosting an observation has a reasonable expectation that you will be in the classroom at the time scheduled. Be sure to arrive on time, step out to debrief on time, and move on to the next classroom on time.

In the five-minute debriefing following an observation, the role of the facilitator is to ask a reflective question related to the best practices just observed in that classroom. Therefore, to be truly authentic, the facilitator is observing for the purpose of planning one to three reflective questions that they will pose to the group once they exit the classroom. (More information on this is in chapter 3.)

Upon leaving the classroom, the teachers involved in the observation will have a brief conversation about the positive aspects of what they observed. At my school, a list of possible questions is shared with all staff at the beginning of each year before our first instructional rounds. Each year the list is updated to include the things we are working on and focusing our professional development around. In the hallway, after observation, the facilitator chooses and asks the debriefing questions. The following are examples of the types of questions the facilitator might ask.

- What were the student learning targets? What evidence of student learning did you see?
- Which of these four PLC questions did you see in action in this classroom?
    - What do we want students to know and be able to do?
    - How will we know if they know it?
    - What do we do when they have not learned it?
    - What do we do when they already know it?
- How did the teacher and the students create or contribute to a safe and supportive learning environment?
- What techniques were used to engage students? How can we tell they were engaged?
- As you think of Webb's Depth of Knowledge, what level of learning was evident?
- What Essential Literacy Practices did you see evidence of?
- Did you observe any teaching or engagement techniques that promoted learning?

- What types of restorative practices did the teacher use to redirect disengagement or off-task behaviors?
- What types of formative assessment techniques and interventions/modifications did the teacher use when the class or a child was not learning the intended target?
- How did the teacher promote connecting students to the learning process?
- As you walked the perimeter of this classroom, what did you notice about the learning in this classroom?
- What did you see that supports the four Cs of twenty-first-century learning—communication, collaboration, critical thinking, and creativity?

The location of the debriefing conversation—in the hallway outside the classroom—is very intentional. During the debriefing conversation, students, other staff, and even parents may walk by. Since all agreements about positivity are always honored, open conversation is appropriate and serves as a structural reminder that the process is safe, trustworthy, and transparent.

Another deliberate action of trust is when the facilitator takes care to make sure that the door of the classroom just visited is open during the debriefing conversation. If it won't stay open on its own, find something to prop it with or stand at the door holding it open with your foot. This minor act is simply an unspoken message of trust. The only times I have allowed the door to be closed is when the teacher or a student from that classroom chose to close the door after we began our conversation.

The Debrief

The group gathers once more immediately after the four observations and debriefing sessions for further personal and collaborative reflective conversation about individual and school-wide instructional practices and their impact on student learning. During this time, the facilitator poses additional reflective questions for each observer to consider before sharing their response with the team. These summarizing questions are an important part of the self-reflection process and are designed to validate and celebrate current effective practices as well as stimulate new questions or new strategies the observing teacher can explore and apply in their classroom for their own professional growth.

Question 1: As a result of what I saw and heard today, which aspects of my own teaching and its impact on student learning do I feel were validated?

The purpose of question 1 is to have teachers reflect in a manner that requires them to compare the practices of their colleagues to their own instructional practices and identify something within their own teaching that they feel is having a positive impact on the learning of their students.

The following are sample responses to this type of question:

> I have been strategic about making sure my students have intentional expectations during Read to Self time this year by setting up each child with a strategy related to their reading goal. When I saw that both Krissy and Karen have differentiated Math Workshop goals and accountability measures in place, it really validated the work I am doing with my students.

> I noticed that when Kristin did a Number Talk with her class she really had to probe and scaffold support for the second student that shared her mathematical strategy. Since the student had the wrong solution, the scaffolds Kristin used supported the student in the self-discovery of her conceptual error. One thing I feel good about today is the way I have been probing my students' thinking to identify if their mathematical errors are due to a simple calculation error or misconception of a mathematical concept. The way I scaffold a child is different depending on the type of error they made.

> We have all been working on responding effectively to student misbehavior this year. I noticed that when Darlene was teaching a small group and a student

> started verbalizing inappropriate phrases from across the room she gave her small group a practice task to work on while she approached the student, knelt down, and whispered something in the student's ear. Darlene walked away and whispered something in the ears of two other students before rejoining her group to continue teaching. Yesterday I tried that same strategy with one of my challenging students, and the student shared with me that he was having a problem with a peer in the class that I was completely unaware of. This has really validated for me that when I invest the time in relationships I have fewer disruptions, and it is paying off by saving me the stressful time I spend handling bigger problems later.

Question 2: As a result of what I saw and heard today, what questions do I have about teaching and its impact on learning that I need to explore further? Or what new ideas do I have to promote high levels of learning in my classroom?

The purpose of question 2 is for teachers to reflect on opportunities for personal growth as an educator and verbalize an action they will take for their own growth and development. This question challenges the observing teachers to reflect on an area they identified as an opportunity for their own professional growth as a result of comparing their practices to the practices of the colleagues they observed. The teachers have two directions they can choose from to determine their next growth steps. Perhaps they have a question resonating in their head that they want to explore through professional conversation with one of the observed teachers, by researching and reading more on a topic, or by eliciting the support of other respected professionals in the field. The second direction the teachers may choose for their personal growth may be to take a new idea they observed in a colleague's classroom and apply it in their own setting with their own students.

The following are sample responses to this type of question:

> When I saw Karen do inside-outside circles with her fourth graders in order to set up collaboration with several peers in the classroom, I started to think about how I can simplify it and do it with my young-fives students. I think I can give each student a card that has a shape and a specific color on it. When I ask them to go to the shape groups, they will group by common shape and talk about the prompt. Then I can ask them to go to their color group, and they will have a new group to collaborate with. I hope this can increase our collaboration and deepen our thinking. I am going to try it this afternoon!

> Today when we walked into Bethany's room, there was a feeling of calm and focus. In my classroom I don't feel this. The question that is rumbling around in my head is, How did she create that feeling of focused calm in her classroom, and how can I work to create the same thing in my room?

> I have been using Number Talks for a while now with my students, and I do see my students benefiting from increased communication about their math thinking, a greater number sense, and increased mental math fluency. But when I saw Courtney's students actually doing their own Number Talks in small groups during Math Workshop I was so impressed. What a great way to give the students autonomy over their own learning and increase the benefits of Number Talks! I want to

> do this with my students, but first I need to sit down with Courtney and learn about how she taught it to the children so that they were ready to take it on independently. The children were very confident and successful in their Number Talks.
>
> When Tiffany questioned her fifth graders about what might have been different if Paul Revere had not made it to the village to warn the residents that the British were coming, the students responded simply at first, but with more time they took it much further. The students began telling stories of alternate versions of what our world may be like today had that moment not happened the way it did. I realized that raising depth of knowledge is not difficult, but it does require that you plan and prepare for these kinds of questions ahead of time. I also realize that when you give kids more time to collaborate on a big question they will move into deeper conversations.

After the observers share their responses to the growth-designed reflection questions, the facilitator as well as other participants will talk about their ideas. Besides encouraging the educators' next steps, the group may also offer ideas, resources, tools, references, and more, all of which the educators can seek out to support their next actions. It's also important to note here that, while we gather plenty of ideas from the four colleagues we observe during an instructional rounds session, each observer will verbalize only *one* thing that they are making a commitment to—whether it is to further explore or learn about a process they plan to pursue or to apply a new idea in their own setting. One goal is more likely to be started right away and accomplished. Having more than one goal may compromise execution, commitment, or success.

Immediate Impact: Support and Implementation

One of the things I enjoy most when leading instructional rounds is taking a group of teachers on instructional rounds in the morning, having them verbalize a strategy they plan to implement in their classroom after being inspired by a colleague, then having them try it immediately in their classroom that day. This actually happens quite often. Oftentimes, they are host teachers for afternoon instructional rounds, and they purposefully try the new strategy when we visit. Seeing this happen reinforces to me that the process is safe and nonthreatening. I am proud that the culture of instructional rounds, when set up to embrace positivity while encouraging growth and professional learning in a risk-free, safe, and supportive system, promotes taking risks even in the presence of an adult audience in the classroom.

(Card by Nancy Colflesh, 2007)

Before the observing teachers return back to their classrooms for the day, as the facilitator, I remind them to write a note to each host teacher to provide them with specific, positive feedback. I keep plenty of note cards available to staff in the PLC room (or staff room) for their use. There are two purposes for this. First, it provides feedback to the host teachers from each observer. Second, this small action contributes to the positive nature of instructional rounds and makes the desire to participate contagious among your staff. Imagine being a teacher and going to your mailbox to find there are four to six cards in there from your colleagues and your principal (or another leader/facilitator). As you open each card, you read specific positive remarks about your teaching and the impact it had on the learning of your students! When I walk through classrooms, it is not unusual to see these note cards stacked neatly on the teachers' work spaces, posted near their computers, or used as bookmarks in their professional resources. In addition to being a technique for providing feedback, the note cards are very special to the recipient. This is truly a gift to our host teachers. As the school leader, I realized these note cards had become a gesture of appreciation between the teachers. Until you see your colleagues teach, you may not know their strengths, or worse, you may make unfair judgments about them. Our school culture had grown into one of appreciation for each other and greater unity. These simple note cards reinforce this appreciation and strengthen our internal network.

When executed to intentionally balance the needs of the feeling brain and the thinking brain, instructional rounds can be the most powerful professional development and culture building experience for a school. The feeling brain relies on the safety nets provided by the premeeting message and statement of the professional agreements, the open location of each observation discussion right outside the classroom door, and the feel-good response when the hosts read the validating note cards they receive from each of the observers after the day has ended. Once it feels safe, the thinking brain is able to reflect, process, contemplate, and learn in classrooms as the teachers observe their peers teach and engage with students. Feeling safe allows the observer to dive into rich conversations following each observation and then develop and share big ideas of validating practices and next steps for growth in the final debriefing conversation. As you prepare to launch instructional rounds at your school, consider the emotional needs of your adult learners so that they can truly reflect on their own teaching and grow.

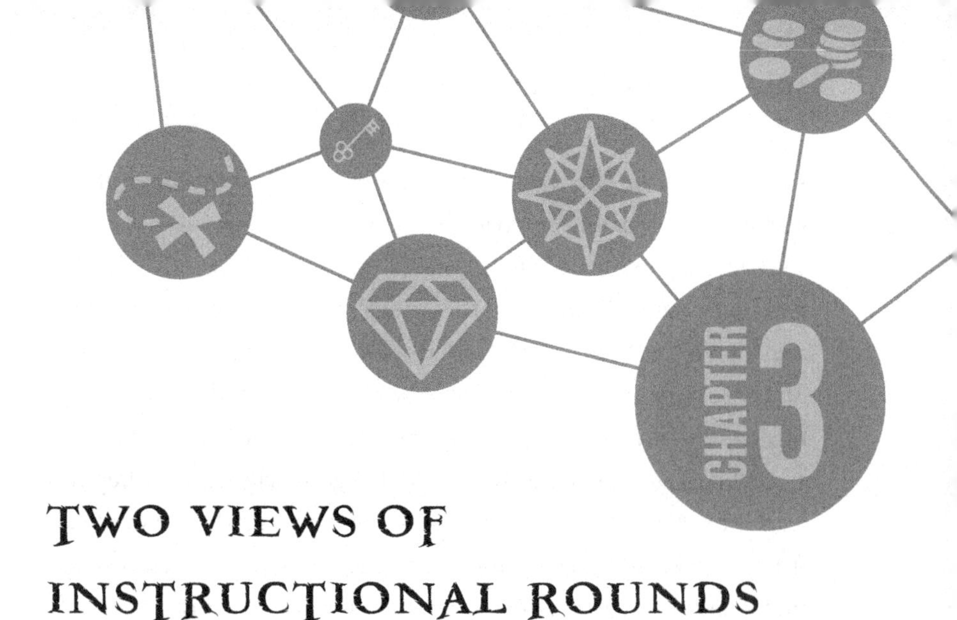

TWO VIEWS OF INSTRUCTIONAL ROUNDS

There are two very different lenses being looked through when doing instructional rounds: the lens of the observing teacher and the lens of the facilitator. While the visiting teachers are observing in order to improve their own teaching practices, the facilitator is observing to identify a few reflective questions that will take the group into a rich and deep conversation about best practices in education.

The observing teachers are looking at what the students are doing and looking for evidence of learning while they are in a host's classroom for rounds. If the class is not engaged in direct instruction at that time, the observers may get down at a child's level and ask specific questions related to learning, purpose, and expectations. The observers will also look at the deliberate actions, movement, and words of the host teacher and the impact those actions have on the students. Additionally, they also look at the walls of the classroom, the artifacts, and the tools available to students in order to analyze the influence that the environment and resources available to the students have on the teacher's instruction as well as on the students' learning and learning behaviors.

As they are observing, teachers are engaged in self-reflection and metacognition. They are thinking about what they see, and they are applying it to the work they are doing with their own students. They are personally evaluating the work they do in their own classroom while they watch their colleague teach. It doesn't matter if it's a second-grade teacher observing a fifth-grade classroom. They will learn just as much from a colleague in a different grade as they would from a colleague teaching the same grade. Research-based instructional best practices are not age or grade specific. Best practices apply to all ages. With instructional rounds, applying practices to another grade level became easier than we first anticipated.

For example, after a young-fives teacher observed the fourth-grade teacher doing inside-outside circles, she immediately set up color and shape cards to help her students match up with talking

partners. Inside-outside circles is a strategy the teacher used to give her fourth graders multiple collaboration partners. In her lesson, she wanted the students to explain a math strategy and justify it to several peers. This strategy was an instructional tool for engagement and collaboration. When the young-fives teacher watched the fourth graders use a procedure to collaborate with multiple partners in a planned, structured, and organized way, she considered how she could achieve that same goal with an age-appropriate procedure with her children. She decided to give each young-fives student an index card. Each card had a shape, had a numeral or dot pattern, and was created with a marker of a certain color. There was another student in the room with their same shape, a different student with a dot pattern to match their numeral, and a third student who also had a card created with the same color. Now the young-fives teacher could prompt the kids to find their shape partner, their number partner, or their color partner in order to have three partners in the room for collaborative conversation.

• • • •

As instructional rounds became a norm in our school, a group of adults walking into a classroom had little to no bearing on the children or the host teacher. I recall a time when a school board member from our district joined me and four teachers on an instructional round. We entered a classroom in which a third-grade teacher was working with a small group of students at a table for a guided reading group, and the rest of the students were engaged in their choice of independent reading, partner reading, word work, or writing. One third grader had selected a cozy spot on the floor right next to the threshold of the entrance so that he could lean against the cupboard with his legs straight out in front of him, crossed at the ankle. A group of five of us entered the classroom, and each one of us stepped over the legs of this independent reader.

A few minutes into our ten-minute observation the school board member whispered to me, "Did you notice the student at the door didn't look up from his book as each one of us stepped over his legs coming into the room? How can that happen?"

When it becomes standard practice and the children know and understand we are coming in to look at teaching and learning in the school so that we can become better teachers, they learn to continue the work they would naturally be doing in the classroom. I also believe they feel proud knowing that grown-ups are visiting to learn from them and their teacher. Our fifth graders that have been with us since kindergarten have only experienced school with monthly visits from professionals to learn about improving teaching and learning. It is the way we work. It is now embedded into our school's culture.

For another example, March is Reading Month, and I am sometimes contacted by a state representative requesting to read to a couple of classes. In this case, the request was made to read to kindergarten. I set the visit up, time passed, and the date finally came. The state representative arrived. I greeted her and walked her down to Krissy's kindergarten classroom. When we arrived, the children were working on their task. Krissy said hello to us and within a few minutes asked the children to clean up and come to the carpet. The state representative and I watched and waited while the children gathered. Once settled, Krissy began the introduction to her next lesson.

Feeling a bit awkward, I interrupted the teacher and her students and introduced the state representative who came to read a story to the class to honor the importance of reading. Once the introductions were made and the guest began reading, Krissy shared that she was sorry she had forgotten. She explained that when she saw me walk in with an adult she (and the children) figured it was an educator from outside our building learning about and experiencing instructional rounds. She carried on as she normally would in a typical day.

My perspective was that her apology, while kind and thoughtful, was completely unnecessary. I felt tremendous pride in that moment. My staff trusted and respected this process enough to see me walk into their room with an adult they did not know and assume it was related to instructional rounds. I was even more impressed that not a beat was skipped by the teacher or the children, especially when they were under the impression that this visit was unplanned and unscheduled. There are rare moments when everything feels right in the world. This was one of those moments. Our culture of instructional rounds was healthy and natural. I was happy and proud. I knew we had come along way.

• • • •

The lens of the facilitator is very different than the lens of the teacher during instructional rounds. The facilitator is using the ten minutes in the classroom to develop a plan for the five minutes that will happen next in the hallway debriefing. To be more specific, I am planning one, two, or three strong questions that will initiate the conversation the group will have in the hallway. I cannot prepare the debriefing questions before the observation because the conversation will not be genuine to the experience we just had. It simply will not be meaningful. My preparation has to be in the moment.

I am already aware of the experience, strengths, and growth needs of my observers. This knowledge is already rumbling around in my head before I enter the first classroom. When I enter a classroom and begin observing, my head is bouncing between thinking, planning, thinking, planning, thinking, and planning in search of opportunities for meaningful reflective questions that will take the group into rich discussion in the hallway. It goes something like this:

> What are the children doing? What is the purpose of their work? Where is the learning target, and how does it give me greater insight to the learning and purpose? What are the children saying? What is the teacher saying or doing? What positive impact do the words, actions, gestures, movement, and location of the teacher have on the students and their learning? What best practices are apparent? What are the strengths of this host teacher? How is the teacher supporting students academically, socially, or behaviorally? Which strengths may be a support to a growth opportunity for the observers? Which strengths contribute to our school-wide growth opportunities and needs? I see a couple of teachers looking at and talking about things on the wall. What is drawing their interest? In what way can I work their interest into a growth opportunity for these observers? Oh yeah, I need to get some pictures of learning to share on Twitter to honor this teacher and promote this work. What time is it? We have two minutes left. I think I have two powerful questions and one extra mediocre question in case I need it.

I never need to use that extra question, yet I always plan it. Collaborative educators will go far with your good questions. Once I ask a good question, the teachers take it from there, and I chime in to clarify, to reinforce, or to contribute to learning conversations only if needed.

If you visit our school to participate in instructional rounds with us, it may look like a well-oiled machine or a beautifully orchestrated cold read. It didn't start that way. We grew into that. I grew as a leader. I distinctly remember, in the beginning, sharing with my staff in the premeeting chat that in the debriefing I would fumble a lot and that my questions would be awkward. I was committed to learning to become smoother. I asked them for their patience and help so I could get better at leading them. It was really awkward at first, and no one was surprised. I fumbled, and my teachers were patient. I was vulnerable. My vulnerability created trust. Trust, camaraderie, and opportunity drew them in.

• • • •

I am the facilitator at my school, but does the facilitator have to be the school principal? No. Any member of your team can facilitate instructional rounds.

Last year, another school visited us and joined in our instructional rounds with the intention of starting a similar process in their own school. The group included four teachers (two of which served as school-improvement leaders in their building), the principal, and the superintendent. When we had completed our full round that day, they asked me if it had to be the principal who facilitates and leads this process. The question surprised me because I had been the only person to lead rounds at my school at that point, so I hadn't given it much thought. After considering the question, I finally replied, "The facilitator should be a person that has ample, current knowledge of best practices of teaching and learning. The facilitator should be respected by the staff and be seen as a person who is trustworthy so that the teachers' need for trust will be honored and the teachers will feel safe throughout the process. To be most effective in using the process to develop individualized teacher development as well as school-wide growth, the facilitator should know the observers as educators and have a sense of their strengths as well as their growth opportunities or needs. The facilitator should also know the school's improvement goals and be involved in current learning and development of the staff."

My learning that day, as I reflected with this visiting school, was that the principal does not have to lead instructional rounds. In fact, there are schools where the principal would not be the most effective person to lead, and a teacher leader, a school-improvement leader, a coach, or a trusted senior colleague would better execute and implement this process in their school. Consider your school dynamics and the people in your school as you choose the right leader or leaders to facilitate this work.

LET'S TALK MONEY AND PARTICIPATION

Without a doubt, instructional rounds are one of the most powerful and cost-effective professional-development experiences for teachers. It also encourages immediate practice and implementation by teachers and brings lasting change.

In our first year, we scheduled instructional rounds once a quarter. The next year, we started in October and did them monthly through May. That worked well—except for May. I learned teachers are not in a good headspace for instructional rounds in May. I should have known better. May is heavy with assessments, end-of-year preparation, and survival! The next two years, we had instructional rounds once a month from October through April. Then one August day, as we were getting ready for a new school year, I suggested to staff we add a September date. Sixteen teachers stared at me with that deer-in-the-headlights look. I smiled and said, "Listen, we have been doing this for a few years now, and we have learned to take risks and to trust and respect the imperfections of ourselves and each other. It has always been safe. Wouldn't it be a great gift to each other to see how we work with students to create our classroom communities and set up our management systems, expectations, and routines? Wouldn't we all benefit from learning from each other in this way? Do you think it will make us better?" And with that, we added September rounds and have continued in that way since.

Each day of instructional rounds I do two sessions: one in the morning and one in the afternoon. This allows for eight teachers to participate in rounds as observers. The expense is simply the cost of substitute teachers needed to release teachers so that they can go on rounds. Budgeting is dependent on the number of subs you decide to hire to release teachers and the number of times you do instructional rounds in a year. At my school, the cost for one year of instructional rounds is the price of thirty-two full-day subs (four subs a month for eight months).

Having student teachers in your school adds cost-free slots for instructional rounds. Each classroom that has a student teacher can be set up so that the student teacher participates as an observer in one rounds session while their assigned teacher stays back to teach the class. In the other session, the student teacher can lead the class on their own while the cooperating teacher joins in on rounds. This is a win-win for everyone, as you don't need a sub to cover that class and more teachers can participate. Additionally, the student teachers get to observe several other teachers and grade levels, have opportunities to have collaborative conversations with experienced educators about the impact of practices they see being implemented in classrooms, and are provided with rich and reflective professional development.

Our school is a Title I school. Since instructional rounds are professional development, we are able to write this practice into our district-improvement plan and use Title II funds to cover the costs of substitute teachers. This is an added benefit to us, but even if we could not charge the cost to Title funds, it is a small price to pay for such a valuable opportunity.

A full instructional-round session lasts approximately one hour and thirty minutes from premeeting to final reflection questions, and we do two sessions in a day. This leaves other opportunities for teacher release that would also require hiring subs, such as mentoring of new teachers, PLC-team release, school-improvement work, meeting attendance, etc.

Voluntary Participation

You will recall that when we defined what instructional rounds are and are not, we decided participation would be voluntary. While it is not required at our school, I am happy to share that *all* of our teachers participate in rounds.

So how do you make it voluntary and still get 100 percent participation? I attribute our success to the way we built a positive culture around instructional rounds, but it was not automatic, and it did take time. Deliberate conversations, assurances of trust, observations, encouragement, and celebrations of the learning and growth through instructional rounds created a process that everyone wanted to get involved with. Some teachers needed more time and encouragement than others; but when their time was right, when the trust was there, they joined in.

Earlier, I shared how our first instructional rounds were conducted on a day we had a staff meeting and that I planned two agendas for that meeting. My hope was that our first rounds would be a fantastic experience and that we would dedicate that staff meeting to hearing about them from the perspectives of those that observed classrooms, followed by the perspectives of the teacher hosts who opened their classrooms to visitors. I had a whole different agenda unrelated to instructional rounds ready for execution in case the experience didn't go as planned. Thankfully, our first rounds were a wonderful experience, and we dedicated that staff meeting to sharing the feelings we had and what we learned. Comments such as these were shared:

> Today as an observer, I saw four of my colleagues in different grades all teaching Math Workshop. There were similarities of each having minilessons and then releasing students into a choice math activity to practice skills either independently or with a partner. It was great to see how they each organized their math-games space and how they each transitioned from a lesson to a workshop choice.
>
> I noticed in Shelby's classroom that the students who played a math game took a place mat they called a work mat with them. When they rolled the dice it had to stay on the work mat to count, and the roll of dice on the soft surface kept the learning environment quiet.
>
> I had no idea how as a fifth-grade teacher I would get so many great ideas from the first- and second-grade classrooms, such as to how to set up my math manipulatives and involve the students in the organization and cleanup of stuff. Today I learned a lot about materials management that I will implement tomorrow in my classroom.
>
> Today when I listened to Nicole's kindergarten students use math talk in their partner work and games, I was so impressed by the amount of math vocabulary they were using in conversation. I realized that I need to raise my expectations for the use of math vocabulary with my upper-grade students.

Imagine you were one of those host teachers hearing these comments. How would you feel? In our meeting that day and in that moment, they felt very proud. And then it was their turn to share their experiences.

> When the group first came in, I felt a little nervous. My students knew they were coming and they continued working as if the visitors were invisible, just as I asked them to. I took a deep breath, focused on my students, and—quite honestly—I forgot they were there very quickly. I continued working with my students, and before I knew it, the ten minutes were up and the group left. I felt good for taking the risk. Now, hearing the positive comments from my colleagues today feels incredible. I would definitely host again. I am proud of the work I am doing.

> I am not used to a group coming in to observe while I teach, but it was surprisingly not uncomfortable. The group moved about the room, looked at the work the students were doing, and asked them questions about their learning. I could tell you were enjoying the students and what was happening in my classroom, so it felt much better than I expected.

You will recall one of our agreements for promoting the positive experience of this process was that each observer would write a note to each teacher they observed that day to express a positive impact this teacher had made on their growth as a teacher. Within the next couple days, each host teacher would receive four to six cards sharing positives about their teaching. This small but simple act is one of the most powerful ways to reinforce instructional rounds in a school and make participation not only continue but spread contagiously.

• • • •

In an article about school reform, Phillip Schlechty describes five roles people play in the change process. Leaders can benefit from recognizing each role that members of their team play and seeing the change as a process that needs to (and will) evolve. I've adapted Schlechty's model in order to describe the five roles I've seen members of my teams play as we build toward change:

1. Architects are risk-takers who are excited to make something new. Once they've found their inspiration, they can easily envision how change will leave the world transformed. They aren't necessarily concerned with the nitty-gritty process of how change takes place, but they're excited to break ground and make a difference.
2. Builders also take risks, and their initiative is rooted in a commitment to community. Inspired by the clear vision of the architects, builders adopt a can-do attitude that inspires others to join the cause of building toward change.
3. Residents will go along with the process of change so long as they understand the reason, purpose, or need for it. Because they're more concerned with process and the long-term sustainability of the project, they like to know what is expected of them, and they need assurance that plans are yielding the results they should.
4. Neighbors don't actively participate in the process of building change, but they also don't challenge it and might actually enjoy it—from a distance. Effective leaders will recognize that neighbors just aren't ready to "make a home" in the shaky new status quo that changes will yield. However, leaders can also rest assured that, with careful planning, the finished product will be welcoming to everyone.

5. Nay-sayers are actively against change and work to stop others from building toward it. They are also risk-takers, but their risk is to undermine the change initiative. Leaders need to keep nay-sayers close so that they can anticipate critiques and build a stronger foundation for change.

In our implementation of instructional rounds, it was the architects, builders, and perhaps a few residents (influenced by builders) that participated in our first few instructional rounds. After that, more residents joined in for the purpose of skill development once they were fully certain there would be no negative consequences of their participation.

Looking back at the launch of our instructional rounds, I cannot identify a single nay-sayer. You will recall that we had nay-sayers on staff prior to this initiative, so why didn't we have them for instructional rounds? Was it because it was, and always would be, voluntary with no pressure to join in? I've also thought that it might be because negative talk was not permitted, and the participants were true to that agreement. This was all about risk-free teacher development, which meant looking for positives.

Two years after our first instructional rounds, I can remember sitting down with Darlene—a teacher who I had unfairly considered a neighbor teacher in rounds. I was quite surprised she hadn't shown any interest yet in jumping on board, because Darlene was always happy, kind, vulnerable, and positive. Everyone on staff loved her. It puzzled me that she never volunteered. After a formal principal observation in Darlene's class one day, I sat with her to dialogue about her lesson and share feedback. After discussing the lesson, I expressed to Darlene that she had a lot to offer her colleagues through her instructional methods, rapport and connection with students, and transitions. I also told her that she would really enjoy seeing the work of her colleagues. I shared that it sometimes helps to experience instructional rounds first as an observer before opening your classroom. I told her that instructional rounds would be a great way to share her expertise with others when the time was right. I then clarified that I would not direct her to participate, but I wished that she would consider it, as she had great strengths to share. She would also enjoy the closeness she could get from seeing her peers teach. Her response was nothing that I expected. It went something like this:

> I know I would enjoy going on instructional rounds. It looks awesome and I have wanted to for a while. I am just not ready to open my classroom yet. I don't know why, but I am really nervous. It doesn't feel right to "get" things from my colleagues when I am not ready to "give" of myself to them. So, I haven't volunteered for either observing or hosting a round.

I knew at that moment I needed to give Darlene an accommodation, just as we would for a student in our class. I replied:

> I understand what you are saying, and I respect your position. I also want to make sure you are growing, and this is a great way to grow with colleagues. I hear that you want to participate in rounds and that you are not ready to open your room as a host. I think that is perfectly normal. I believe that once you see how casual and positive it is, it will not seem nearly as scary to open your room. Therefore, I have a special rule I am requiring of *you*. You are not allowed to open your classroom to visits until you have participated as an observer in at least four instructional rounds. It can be more than four, but it cannot be less than four. If and when you are ready to be a host, I will happily accept you in that role. But first you must observe four or more rounds.

For a moment, Darlene tried once more to say it is not fair to get something without giving something. I repeated the rule of four observations and reminded her that "fair is not equal. This is what you need." After her first instructional round as an observer, Darlene was beyond excited. She immediately put things into practice later that day. Darlene did the next three instructional rounds in a row and then volunteered to be a host. She was nervous, but she taught and connected to kids in the amazing way I had experienced when I had been in her room. She showed her strengths with her teacher friends, and they were also impressed. Darlene confessed that when we came in, she just "taught on." In the beginning, she had no idea who entered the room because looking up at the visitors made her nervous. Today, it is second nature. She welcomes visits from guests in our school as well as external districts. I have been so proud to see her journey. Before I had that feedback meeting with Darlene, I would have said she was a neighbor type. I learned that she was a resident. She wanted to make the journey, but she needed a builder to lead her down the path. Residents do not all immediately follow. They do it at their own pace, and they may need a builder to seek them out and support their growth.

The following seven tips suggest ways a leader can support participation in instructional rounds without making it required.

1. Most importantly—uphold the positivity of all talk related to instructional rounds. Trust is critical to participation.
2. Be sure to emphasize the importance of writing feedback on note cards to host teachers. Provide note cards to the observers after the rounds debriefing session.
3. Offer professional-development hours for participating teachers so they can use the hours toward their certificate renewal or for required new-teacher-development hours (if eligible in your state).

4. New teachers coming into an existing culture of instructional rounds may eagerly participate. Make sure you make them feel invited and included.
5. Write instructional rounds participation in individualized development plans for teachers on an improvement plan. This is the only time I require participation in instructional rounds and it is appropriate. Instructional rounds are a powerful improvement tool for struggling teachers.
6. Invite them. It's okay to invite a teacher to participate. An invitation is not a mandate.
7. When someone volunteers, always say yes!

What if a teacher volunteers who may not have the strengths you are currently trying to grow in your staff? Or worse, what if a teacher volunteers, and you are uncertain what their strengths are? If you are going to honor all of your staff and build a learning culture with all-inclusive instructional rounds, then you need to always say yes!

I remember going on rounds during a time that our staff was working on shifting our practices to twenty-first-century learning. We were working on including a high degree of student choice and voice, collaboration throughout the school day, communication opportunities for students, critical thinking at differentiated levels, and creativity woven throughout the learning progression. One month, a teacher opened her classroom for rounds. When we entered, the room was quiet, as all the students were working on a math sheet. Each student had the same math worksheet, and the desks were set up in rows. Students were each working independently. I realized immediately I could not pose a question to support our pursuit of twenty-first-century learning.

As the leader, I now had nine minutes of observation time to think of a debriefing question that would highlight a strength of this teacher so that my observing teachers could grow from this observation and my host teacher could feel strengthened. I reflected on the strengths of this teacher and realized that she had a gift of connecting to kids and building a rapport with silliness and motherly expectations. These special interactions happened with incredible ease and were a daily continual communication she had with her students. The children enjoyed her because she connected with them and she was age-appropriately funny. They rose to her expectations because they liked her. During the next eight minutes, I noticed that as she moved within the rows of desks she interacted with every student and made connections. Some connections were helpful engagement with their work, while other contacts were simply to share humor.

Stepping out into the hallway, we talked about the power of relationships. Our conversation was positive, and everyone learned something valuable to reflect on. I do believe that all educators bring themselves to the classroom in ways that don't always show up in the latest list of generic best practices. A school leader should always be open to seeing this reality in their teachers.

Build commitment to the instructional rounds process and weave it into the culture of your school in a way that brings a feeling of learning, growth, positivity, and appreciation for those we work with. You will find that instructional rounds will become the way you do things at your school. Participating becomes the norm, and not participating eventually becomes uncomfortable.

UNINTENDED AND UNEXPECTED SOLUTIONS

Many schools implement instructional rounds by beginning with determining a problem of practice—a high-leverage practice that needs improvement across all levels of the building or system. The specific purpose of identifying a system-wide problem of practice, either in a school or a district, is to create systematic change in the organization around those practices to address that recognized problem. I can tell you that our school certainly has problems of practice, however, in the protocol we use, we do not identify a focal problem to concentrate our observations on.

One approach to instructional rounds begins with a designated leadership team conducting a school walk-through, similar to an audit, in which they look for a problem of practice to focus the school's improvement efforts on. Instructional rounds are then executed specifically to look for the identified problem of practice, followed by discussions about the best practice to make systemic improvements in that focused need. As I was reading all the research and books I could find about instructional rounds, I knew I had to steer away from focusing on problems of practice. Trust and vulnerability were broken at Monroe. We needed to heal. We needed to see and learn to respect the individual strengths every member of our school had to offer. We needed to become a culture that put away the sense of threat permanently and become a new team. We needed to learn to love (or at least appreciate) each other. For our school to heal and grow as a team that respected and appreciated one another, we needed to look for strengths in each one of us and tie those strengths to best practice to help each of us grow from what each teacher had to offer. Initially, I wasn't looking for instructional rounds to bring systemic growth and building-wide implementation of best practices. I was looking to improve each teacher personally and professionally and to build a strong and respectful school culture.

A magnificent thing happened. By staying true to our "the answer is in the room" intention of implementing instructional rounds and focusing on teacher development through reflection, metacognition, and collaborative conversation, each participant got what they *needed* rather than what a school leadership team deemed everyone would observe and improve in. I realized my teachers were getting differentiated and personalized development. Additionally, the invisible wall separating the McKinley teachers and the Monroe teachers began to crumble. Each participant had strengths that led to exciting conversations about best practices in teaching and learning. When we entered a classroom together, there was no indication that this was a certain type of teacher—the "McKinley type" or the "Monroe type." We began to see each other through the strengths each person offered and not through the differences that created that sense of threat we felt back when we merged two very different schools together. We grew individually and we grew as a team by observing each other.

This is a good time to point out the benefit of having a facilitator, whether it's the school principal or another leader in the school, who thoroughly knows the strengths and growth opportunities of each teacher in the school. When I take a small group of newer teachers on instructional rounds, I often look for opportunities to ask questions on effective management and show ways the host teacher has built a strong community of learners. In another round, I may have a teacher in the group who I know has set a goal that year to increase rigor through high-level questioning. And in an observation, I may see a host teacher present a deep question to her class and prompt them to turn and deliberate over the question. So I will certainly pose a question to that group about ways the teacher took her instruction to depth of knowledge level three (DOK 3). Every observer will learn and grow from that collaborative talk on depth of knowledge, but one teacher will get exactly what she needed with that question. When the facilitator is an instructional leader who knows the staff at this professional level, your rounds will be highly personalized and even more effective for individual teacher development.

School-Wide Professional Development

As we grew into our instructional rounds, another wonderful thing happened. Being the school principal, I was the person making our informed professional-development plans for the year, choosing books and articles to share with my teachers, and outlining our school-improvement plan with my leadership team. None of these decisions happened randomly. In fact, such decisions were made through the examination of data, dialogue, and walking through classrooms. I knew what our problems of practice were. All of us at Monroe knew, because they were what was shaping our school-improvement plan and its goals. Our problems were our learning opportunities and what I planned our professional development around. To improve these learning opportunities, I choose articles and books to share and read together as a staff so that we can build our shared knowledge of new practices together. In fact, I am *always* looking for ways to develop our growth opportunities during rounds by being keenly alert of strong, effective practices in a classroom that address those problems. It just sounds different when I bring it into instructional rounds. Remember, one of our agreements is that we will only speak of the positives, therefore, I need to make sure the language of addressing practices to support our growth areas (or problems) sounds something like this:

> One of the things we have been learning about this year is the CRA approach to support students who are struggling in math. We know we start with concrete (C) development of the concept using manipulatives and tools with kids. When they are solid, we can begin representational (R) interpretation, such as pictures and diagrams. Lastly, we can move kids into abstract (A) math, such as algorithms and paper and pencil tasks. What did you notice the whole class doing today, and in what ways were they successful with it? What did you see Devin, as the teacher, doing with her small group, and what was the impact on students? How did you see deliberate CRA methods being used in this class? What was the impact on individual student learning? What information do you think informed the instructional decisions this teacher made today?

After launching this question, the group would engage in discussion on best practices using the CRA model in their Math Workshop and whole-group / small-group lesson planning.

Here is another way it may sound:

> One of the things we are working on as a whole school right now is to exercise relationship building and prevention strategies to reduce behavior challenges in the classroom. Let's share and talk about the deliberate

> actions we noticed Dana use with her students today that were either relationship building or prevention techniques. What did you observe was the immediate impact on student behavior in each strategy we observed Dana use?

Dialogue on this question would take the group through a review of strategies we had learned to develop deep and meaningful relationships with kids. It would also reinforce the need for conscious prevention actions on the part of the teacher to reduce students' challenging behavior. They would discuss ways their colleague Dana used the strategies effectively and the positive impact these strategies had on her class or an individual student. The debriefing conversation following this reflection question may sound like this:

> Sometimes I get so stressed trying to fit in all of my curriculum in a day that I don't devote time into building the relationships. I noticed that right after she finished her minilesson, Dana sat one-on-one and talked to a student about her pets for a minute or two before starting her first small group. I see how the time is well worth it.
>
> I had the same thought. I also get too focused on meeting my curricular needs, and I lose sight of the student needs. I used to use the two-by-ten strategy with my class, and, for some reason, I have not done it for a while.
>
> Another thing I saw Dana do was deliberately ignoring a student calling out to her while she was instructing. Once she directed the class in the next turn and talk, she had a quick private conversation with that student before listening to some of the other conversations. I remember reading about prevention phrases before.

> During the first days of school, you tell your kids that you will ignore certain things while you are teaching and handle them privately later. Dana handled that wonderfully and with great patience. The students did not respond to the misbehavior, nor did they call their teacher's attention to it.
>
> Each of the students Dana interacted with by relationship building or ignoring and addressing later had no negative impact on the learning of the rest of the kids. Her class trusted she would take care of it when the time was right, and they know that she handles things privately, so they gave no regard to the student's concerns. They all continued to learn.
>
> Also, by being so calm and managing behavior predictably and privately, the students in question were easily addressed and refocused on the right thing, and they were also able to continue learning.

After several years of conducting instructional rounds and reflecting on whether or not to focus on problems of practice, I believe there is an opportunity for a special niche here. I have two recommendations for my colleagues who wish to lead instructional rounds for professional development while simultaneously building and maintaining a positive, supportive culture in their school:

1. Use instructional rounds as a protocol for teachers to engage in reflective thinking and dialogue on what they need right now: their interests, their personalized needs or goals, or their privately identified area of struggle. This reflective thinking makes each teacher's experience and education unique, and it supports personalized teacher development.
2. Be vigilant about looking for experiences in the host classrooms that could build awareness of something important or

inspire reflective strategies for current school-wide professional learning, school-improvement goals, or opportunities for system or school-wide growth. This dialogue advances systemic change in your current initiatives, improves practices in school-wide learning needs and opportunities, or both.

When an instructional rounds facilitator leverages *both* of these opportunities with their debriefing questions, that leader has hit the professional-development jackpot, causing both personalized teacher development as well as systematic school change! I call this the instructional rounds sweet spot.

The Unexpected!

Our initial purpose in instructional rounds was to improve on our own teaching practices by watching our peers teach, reflecting as we observed, and identifying ways we could improve and grow in our own instructional practices.

The first unexpected and immediate benefit was that the structure and process of instructional rounds healed our hurt and broken culture. We were once a culture that was void of trust, and then we found that trust through the process of instructional rounds. The embedded positivity and transparency in the process, the enthusiasm we felt after watching our colleagues teach, and the following dialogue about the positive impact their instructional decisions and student interactions had on learning was exciting. The walls we built up to protect ourselves during the difficult times of challenge, change, and growth began to come down, and we became a team. Negative assumptions were dispelled, as our talk was about strengths in our colleagues. I believe the critical element of our cultural growth developed because of the positive talk and focus on strengths.

There has been much research on the topic of emphasizing employee strengths and weaknesses. Studies indicate that when organizations focused on strengths in their employees, performance rose significantly. Conversely, when organizations focused on weaknesses, performance declined significantly. Strength-related feedback improves goal achievement, loyalty, and employee engagement.

The next unexpected benefit we noticed was the development of a common school language. Having regular professional conversations about teaching and learning led to shared language about instruction, expectations, procedures, and communication throughout our school. This commonality is a benefit to students, parents, and guests to our school, as it limits the likelihood of potential miscommunication and misinterpretation of talk around campus. Visitors to our school have often commented to me, "Everyone in your school all talks the same. You have the same priorities and common language." I am very proud when that comment is made, and they are right—we do. When a school staff regularly engages in conversation about instructional practices in their own and in each others' classrooms, they all begin to talk the same talk and walk the same walk. As the leader as well as a participant, I see my role as making sure those conversations are rooted in research-based best practices.

The third benefit was the development of a shared vision of best practices of instruction, learning, and student support throughout the school. Each time we debriefed after an observation and reflected at the end of an instructional round, we were building our capacity and understanding of best practices in education. Throughout the instructional rounds process, the observing teachers were absorbed in self-reflection of their own practices as they watched their colleagues teach and engage with students. As the facilitator of rounds, I carefully constructed debriefing questions to pinpoint best practices presented and, through conversation, brought awareness of the impact such practices have on student learning.

Another unexpected advantage that we realized after doing instructional rounds was the power of vertical observations—meaning observing colleagues teaching grades above or below the grade level of the observing teachers. This may have been our greatest surprise. Each time we did instructional rounds, teachers reflected on a practice they saw in an alternate grade level that they were excited to immediately apply to their own students. This adaptation makes sense when you think about it, because research-based best practices of instruction apply to all levels of learners. The content should change as you move through various grades, but best practices are ageless. It is not unusual for a third-grade teacher to see a great strategy in action in a kindergarten classroom and then take it to her classroom or share it with her PLC team. Once we discovered the benefit of vertical observations, I became mindful of scheduling the host teachers so that we always had a variety of grade levels represented in our observations.

Recently, our school hosted a visit from high school math teachers. The purpose of this visit was to see how our elementary math instruction was delivered in short minilessons and followed by collaborative or independent practice by students and teacher-led small-group instruction differentiated by student need. I set up the observations instructional rounds style with a variety of primary, middle grade, and upper elementary classrooms included in these visits. I intentionally avoided setting up only upper elementary visits since the ages of those learners were the closest I had to high school students. I wanted the observers to connect the practices in the primary math classroom to the practices of the upper elementary classroom and each grade in between. Before we set off to observe, I reminded the observing high school teachers that best instructional practices apply to all K–12 students. I invited them to reflect on how the practices they saw evident in the classrooms that they visited that day would apply to their high school setting. I was nervous for this rounds session because I was concerned the elementary content would be a huge obstacle to looking deeper at the actual practices that were being used to inform students; evaluate their understanding; and then strategically make decisions designed to support students that needed more time, more practice, or more instruction that may even include prerequisite skills. To my great relief, it was indeed the practices that the math teachers reflected on, and we were able to dive into deep conversation about how they could use many of these practices and lesson structures to meet the needs of their high school math students.

The final benefit I would like to share is that change initiatives in our school went quicker with instructional rounds. Think back to change initiatives you may have experienced in schools you have worked in. It seems like there are always a couple of initiatives happening at all times, and they can often be pretty slow to take off. Have you agreed with a new initiative but perhaps needed some kind of nudge to act? Instructional rounds always serve as that nudge for us. In fact, I have witnessed instructional rounds make new initiatives contagious.

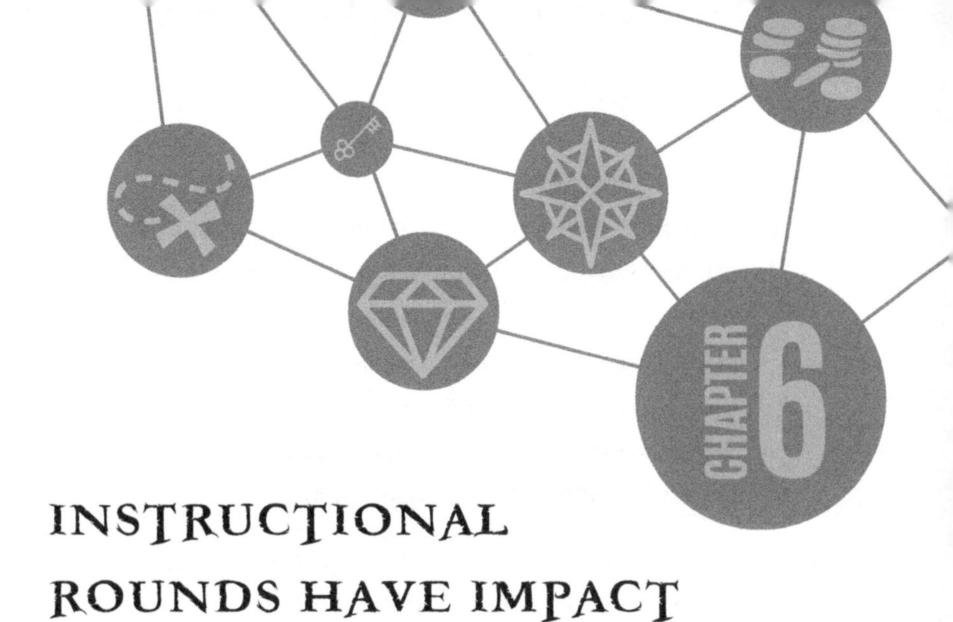

INSTRUCTIONAL ROUNDS HAVE IMPACT

Once the implementation of instructional rounds was underway and it was a regular practice at our school, benefits beyond the initial goals of improving teacher practice and building a positive culture were realized. I started to see how the process could have incredible benefits for new teachers, strengthen the work of our PLCs, and make change initiatives happen with greater clarity and ease. Instructional rounds are a process into which you can apply any context for growing teachers and building your school's culture.

Beginning Teachers

Instructional rounds provide incredible support for new teachers and should be a part of the mentoring process. Participating in instructional rounds immerses new teachers into our school, gives them a broad view of instruction at multiple levels and content areas, and provides ongoing observation, reflection, and dialogue with several professionals.

Based on the work of the National Foundation for the Improvement of Education, the National Education Association (NEA) suggests that beginning teachers should receive three stages of mentoring.

> Stage 1: This stage covers practical skills and information. This includes where to get supplies, how to organize a classroom, instructional resources, and information about the teacher association.
>
> Stage 2: This stage covers the art and science of teaching, and it deals with polishing teachers' classroom management skills.
>
> Stage 3: This stage is for developing a deeper understanding of instructional best practices and includes ongoing professional development based on the needs of their students.

My experience has been that schools often assign a mentor to each new teacher to be their go-to support person. Mentor teachers tend to do a great job fulfilling stage one for the beginning teacher, but often schools do not go beyond stage one in their new teacher mentoring programs. Do those mentor teachers have the means and a system in place to accomplish stage two and stage three singlehandedly? The process of instructional rounds allows the entire staff to embrace our new teachers and plunge into the deeper levels of stage two and stage three of mentoring. Through this collaborative process, the entire school staff can influence and support our new teachers in the final two stages, providing our new teachers with greater and deeper support and development.

Teachers who join our school new to this process have said:

> Participating in instructional rounds as a new teacher gave me classroom management ideas to implement in my own classroom. It was also validating when I saw something posted or something that an experienced teacher was doing that I was doing in my classroom as well!

> As an experienced teacher that moved from a traditional charter school to a public school with a high level of student collaboration and choice, I found instructional rounds to not only be helpful but a necessary part of my learning and growth as an educator. As many of us already know, educators learn the most from each other. Having the time to visit co-workers in action gave me real-life examples of different ways to use flexible seating and other techniques my co-workers were using that I didn't know were out there.

New teachers to our school are eager to jump on board and observe their colleagues through instructional rounds, particularly because it is an embedded practice within the school's culture. My practice has been to meet with new teachers and explain the process of instructional rounds at our school and its benefits. I give new teachers a priority spot as an observing teacher each month. I also suggest that during their first year they only observe, without any pressure to be a host teacher. After year one, new teachers decide for themselves when they want to open their classrooms for their colleagues.

School-Wide Change Initiatives

No one will argue that change is easy. Change within an organization is extremely hard, as each member will have their own unique emotions and perceptions regarding the change initiative. Additionally, if you tend to take on the role of architect or builder, you will react to change differently than residents or neighbors.. Furthermore, the presence of nay-sayers can have a profound negative impact on every person on the team. There is an interdependence of all the members of an organization as they react to and respond to change.

Did I mention change is really hard?

Instructional rounds have been a gift during a few change initiatives we have launched. Exercising instructional rounds has led to quicker than typical change initiatives in our school. Some of these happened intentionally by setting up rounds to explore a pending initiative as our architects and builders jumped in and were ready to try it out first. Remember, architects and builders are comfortable with risk. They will jump in, try it out, *and* let others watch it happen.

For example, we knew we needed to change our intervention practices from pull-out support, where students are pulled out of the classroom to an alternate location, to push-in support, where instructional aides enter the classroom and work with students in their own classroom. When we were ready to make this change, we were also making significant changes in scheduling, classroom-design needs, and the structure of our instructional plans. While all teachers and support staff agreed with the practices we needed to shift to, there were so many changes in structure that it was hard to visualize how to do it.

Kristin and Darlene, our second-grade collaborative team, were our architects in this intentional change process through instructional rounds. You may remember from chapter 4 that Darlene was a resident in instructional rounds participation. This time, with a new initiative, she had become a leader in her own right. Each time we experience a new change initiative, we take on a role that matches our comfort and risk level.

Together with their instructional aides, Sue and Heather, they developed a structure and invited the aides into the classroom for additional small-group interventions. They set up a work space for Heather and Sue to fulfill small-group interventions, while Kristin and Darlene each had their own small group for interventions. Across the grade level, there were four educators doing supplementary interventions at the same time, based on student need. No student had to be pulled out of the classroom to get what they needed, and no student missed core instruction to receive additional time and support in a deficit skill. As soon as Kristin and Darlene had a structure in place, long before it was a well-oiled machine, I asked them to take a risk and volunteer to host instructional rounds just a couple weeks into developing their system.

Because they had taken such confident steps toward change, Darlene and Kristin were sure to set an example that would encourage builders and residents to adopt new practices. Darlene and Kristin agreed, and during instructional rounds that month, the observing teachers who were trying to implement a similar structure were excited and ready to dive in. This particular session of rounds made such an impact that by the end of the week several teachers that didn't go on rounds that day were asking to get in as soon as possible to see how Darlene and Kristin set up their structure. For the next couple of weeks, teachers gave up their prep time or found coverage for their class so they could get in and learn from their second-grade teacher colleagues. On top of that, Kristin, Darlene, and I were getting emails from other schools in the district asking to visit and learn from them.

Kristin and Darlene, with support from Heather and Sue, certainly adopted an innovative practice, and within one month the entire school had developed a push-in intervention structure. When you can see what a new initiative can look like in your own school, have the opportunity to engage in self-reflection as you observe it in action, and then participate in collaborative dialogue about best practices in education, a movement happens. As a seasoned educator, I can honestly say that I have never seen change initiatives happen as fast as I have by making them visible during instructional rounds.

• • • •

Using rounds to introduce that change initiative was very intentional. I would like to share one experience that was not set up or planned for. This was the accidental event that made me realize the power of instructional rounds in supporting change.

As a staff, we had been doing professional learning in our staff meetings about the concept of Number Talks with kids. Number Talks are collaborative talks around a math calculation. The students solve the problem mentally, and then several students share their mental math processing and the solution they came up with. It's an effective approach for developing math fluency, reasoning, strategy, and math communication.

In our meetings, we were exploring this topic and learning about it through video resources and a book study. Even though we saw external videos of educators conducting Number Talks, it was a very slow kickoff in our school. Many months after studying Number Talks and watching videos, we walked into Nicole's kindergarten class one day for instructional rounds. Nicole held up a scatter-dot image and said to her students, "What do you see and how do you see it?" This was followed by incredibly rich conversation about numbers, values, and combinations.

For the first time, we saw our own teacher apply a Number Talk with her students that resulted in rich math talk by students. Every observer that day led their first Number Talk with their class at various grade levels within days of the observation. One actually led her first Number Talk that very afternoon during the second session of instructional rounds for a new group of observing teachers. That second group of observers, in turn, also jumped in to bring Number Talks to their classrooms within the week. It was truly contagious. Within one week, we went from one teacher doing a Number Talk to 50 percent of the staff doing it. Before our next month of instructional rounds, the entire staff had implemented Number Talks in their classrooms. If a teacher didn't see it in action, word of mouth took over, and everyone got what they needed to feel empowered to try it out.

Wearing my facilitator lens as well as my principal lens during instructional rounds, I also have the opportunity to self-reflect on the process. It was this day that I realized the untapped opportunity of instructional rounds in change initiatives. This discovery was a game-changer.

Here is one more example. As a staff, we were studying twenty-first-century learning. Our professional conversations were about student choice and voice, raising the expectations of frequent and rich student collaboration, bringing creativity into the learning experiences, challenging our students to think critically, and learning how to turn the stage over to the students for communicating their learning in a variety of ways.

And then we realized our classroom environments were not all conducive to this kind of learning. Teachers started removing their teacher desks to give more space for collaborative work. Next, student desks were pulled together so groups could have larger work spaces. I remember going into Karen's fourth-grade class for rounds one day, and the student desks were in groupings (which didn't surprise me), but they were turned around backward so the kids could not access the cubby space of the desk. Karen had found alternate spots in the classroom to hold supplies and taught the class to welcome the concept of communal, or shared, supplies. Karen taught her students that "just as a family has a space for pencils, crayons, and scissors that we share, our classroom family will do the same."

Karen taught me the most important reason for flipping the desks around. In order to allow flexible movement in your classroom, you need to transform thinking from "the space I own" to "our classroom is full of work spaces, and this is the space I am using right now." The next day, the proud principal in me bought Karen a few activity tables, and as soon as they arrived, the desks were swiftly replaced.

During our growth into twenty-first-century learning, our instructional rounds process included much talk about learning environments that support twenty-first-century learning. Once again, this was a fast change in our school. This change process I will attribute first to a paradigm shift in which our teachers identified that our learning environments no longer matched our beliefs about learning. When that happens for an educator, you really have no choice but to figure out a new way.

For us, that was flexible seating, and we unanimously decided we would do it school-wide. Again, that happened quickly. This conversation happened at a staff meeting one day in March. Half of the staff decided they would shift to flexible seating immediately after spring break (architects and some builders, for sure), and the rest of the staff decided they would be all-in by September. There were no neighbors or nay-sayers this time. I have often wondered why that was. Was it because we dove so deep into twenty-first-century learning first? Was it because once you truly commit to this type of learning you must have a matching learning environment? Years after shifting our learning environments to match our learning beliefs, our teachers cannot fathom going back.

PLCs

The work of Richard Dufour describes professional learning communities (PLCs) as "an ongoing process in which educators work collaboratively in recurring cycles of collective inquiry and action research to achieve better results for the students they serve. PLCs operate under the assumption that the key to improved learning for students is continuous job-embedded learning for educators." There are three big ideas that drive the work of a PLC:

1. A focus on learning
2. A collaborative culture and collective responsibility
3. A results orientation

The regular practice of instructional rounds embraces this same description as well as the three big ideas that drive PLC work.

A school that operates as an authentic PLC school has teacher teams meeting frequently to establish learning targets, analyze the results of student learning, make plans for intervention and extension, and improve their practices through professional dialogue about the practices that worked or didn't work in their classrooms. The work of a PLC, comprising individual teachers who teach the same grade level or the same course, is powerful. When implemented with strong dedication by the entire team, PLC work yields great results in student achievement.

Now let's pair the dedicated work of a high-performing PLC school with a systematic structure of regular instructional rounds. In this way, the professional conversations can move beyond a roundtable discussion of an individual collaborative team's work to the school-wide, shared work of all PLCs. Our interdependence between grade levels and subject areas becomes apparent, and we can learn from each other more fully. Additionally, we see each other teach, which creates a much deeper level of understanding of the practices we are using and the impacts they are having on student learning. Observation deepens our understanding more than simply trying to explain our instructional practices to our colleagues. Blending instructional rounds with PLC work can leverage amazing adult and student learning for any school.

Our most recent application of instructional rounds was a bit outside of the box. It combined supporting a change initiative and reinforcing the work of a PLC in our school. We have a strong commitment to PLCs, and we continually aspire to grow our practices as a PLC. In our school, like all schools, we have varying degrees of commitment to the process and to the work, which is a growth opportunity. In our school, collaborative teams identify times during the school week that they have common planning availability to dedicate to structured PLC work. Our fifth-grade collaborative team had experienced an epiphany on the work of professional learning communities. As they went through the required protocols and were compliant with the expectations, this team had an aha moment as the big picture suddenly clicked. Compliance was immediately washed away, and true commitment set in. Enthusiasm took over the team and they were rocking the PLC work. Most of our other collaborative teams were not at this level of commitment and enthusiasm.

For several months in a row, our instructional rounds included one visit that was not instructional. The fifth-grade collaborative team was the host while we spent our ten minutes watching them engage in their PLC work during a team meeting. After the ten-minute observation, the observers stepped into the hallway to debrief this team's collaborative work. Some of their reflections included:

> The team is using a consistent protocol to plan their unit, and it flows so well. They have their results prepared and are recording them within their protocol.
>
> The moment that struck me the most was when they reviewed the results of last year's common assessment data. I know that is important, but when they reviewed and talked about the misconceptions the students had last year and how they would plan for them and address them immediately, I was instantly sold as to why we need to record our instructional strategies that worked and didn't work within our protocol. I would never be able to remember details like that from a year ago. That can really save a tremendous amount of instructional time.

This process had great impact as teachers observed and then engaged in PLC work with their own collaborative team. After this observation of our fifth-grade team using their unit protocol, our protocol finally came to life within the other collaborative teams. All our teams grew as a result.

My leadership lesson in this chapter is to be open and alert to the possibilities before you as you continually lead growth in your school. Ask yourself, "Can instructional rounds support our growth and initiate needed change, and how can I work this into instructional rounds to support and benefit my staff, their growth, and our school?"

CONCLUSION

When we began implementation of rounds at Monroe Elementary, my initial hope was to improve teaching and learning at my school and to give teachers a chance to see their colleagues teach so that they could appreciate the strengths each person on our staff brings to their classrooms. Not only was my initial hope realized but the potential for so much more unfolded in this work. While each teacher was building on their own use of best practices in the classroom, school-wide practices and new initiatives began to take seed—quickly. Our teachers had a better understanding of research-based best instructional practices and began to speak with greater confidence about the work they were doing in their classrooms. Their individual efficacy was growing. Our collective efficacy was growing. Classrooms throughout the school applied workshop models of instruction, with student choice and voice prioritized. Desks were moved out and replaced with large open spaces and collaborative work spaces for group work. Discussions about rigor and the common core shifts in English-language arts and mathematics instruction were typical discussions in our school. Students didn't miss a beat when a group of adults walked into their classrooms and watched them work and learn. The practice became embedded into the culture of Monroe while, at the same time, it was forming a culture of professionalism and adult learning at our school. A school that was once broken after a difficult merger involving two opposing entities learned to trust each other. By working together to create a process that was transparent, everyone began to feel safe to participate at their own pace. Our agreements of focusing on the positivity of each other's work helped us to see the strengths every teacher at our school brings to our collective team. We were no longer divided. It brought us unity.

Monroe Elementary School soon identified as a school focused on learning—for both students and adults. Our focus on learning and the dedication we had to it became apparent to me two years after we began instructional rounds. One August afternoon before the new school year started, I had the entire teaching staff at my home for lunch and to have a school-year planning meeting. State assessment scores had just been released, and we were disappointed with our ranking. It was at this meeting that I shared the idea of professional learning communities. I had just attended a PLC institute, and I was aware that the concept would be new to my staff. We were also in a place of urgency with our performance data, and we were a team dedicated to learning. After ample discussion about what professional learning communities did for student learning as well as about the difference between a high performing PLC and a PLC lite, we voted unanimously to start PLC work in our school with a promise that we would not do PLC lite. Having instructional rounds already in place really enhanced the PLC work in our school. Teams were able to move beyond the discussion level of sharing instructional practices that were working or not working with their students to seeing them in full action by observing in each others' classrooms. Observing the work of students in grades above or below brought in the additional element of the effective work on vertical teams in our school as well as the interdependence each grade-level team has on the work of other teams. By having a culture in which we already felt safe watching each other teach, we were already vulnerable enough to share our class data and struggles in a collaborative team meeting. When a team was ready, we brought instructional rounds to a collaborative team meeting instead of to a classroom. I am proud to share that four years after beginning our PLC commitment at Monroe, our school was named a nationally recognized Model PLC School by Solution Tree. I feel this accomplishment had everything to do with our new school culture that was already deeply committed to both adult and student learning. And instructional rounds became a tool to actually observe for ourselves the impact our instruction had on student learning in the classrooms of our school.

Just as my school and staff have grown through this work, I have grown as a leader. Talking with staff about high-leverage instructional practices on a regular basis keeps me on top of my game as an instructional leader. Keeping up with my own professional reading and sharing professional resources with staff is critical. However, I must always be keenly aware to share the right information at the right time, as I don't want to overwhelm my staff. When I give the right information at the right time, it should be embraced and seen as necessary information making things better, not harder. New learning should be connected to the needs teachers have as educators or the needs of their students. I have learned to read the reactions of my staff better, and I know when I have layered too much on them and when it's appropriate to push a little. There is a time and a place for intentional disruption of past beliefs, and I have learned to be strategic and to try to time it wisely. I wish I could say there is a magic formula that tells me when. There isn't. It is more of a trial and error of pushing and pulling back until you find that sweet spot for your staff—just like teachers do to find the appropriate productive struggle for their students to grow to their potential.

I learned, in the early days of McKinley, that I could have a happy staff by not pushing them into discomfort. Then I learned they were not growing to their potential as educators. The circumstances of the merger taught me that when the people of an organization do not have voice or control in their circumstances, factions and sabotage can take root. Second-order change can make people feel as if they have no voice or control. I learned that when I have to lead my school through significant change, I need to find a way to provide a sense of control and voice. I need to find who the architects are in this change and give them the opportunity to lead it. I also need to find the builders, as they will have the strongest voice to influence others in a positive direction. I also need to identify any nay-sayers in the change initiative. Their voices need to be recognized and heard and their concerns identified and worked through. Perhaps they need to lead us through the navigation of the messy problem they are challenged with. I have learned that there is no perfect playbook and that you can start with a vision, develop a plan, and then fly the plane. From my first day as a principal to this moment as I am finishing the last pages of this book, I have grown from a novice principal who felt discomfort with the notion of my position of power into a resilient and respected instructional leader who has, with the support of amazing educators by my side, built a culture of professional learners.

Like any reflective learner, as I look back on my journey with instructional rounds and leadership, there are things I would have done differently. The first and foremost thing that comes to mind is that hesitation I had in launching our first instructional rounds. I allowed my fear of failure during a difficult time in my school to hold me back from just flying the plane. I was holding my whole school back from growing professionally and growing together. Would we have become the school we are today sooner if I had just flown the plane despite my fear? When we began our PLC journey after our school culture had already become both collaborative and learning focused, I was like a broken record to my collaborative teams, saying, "Just fly the plane. Let it crash. See what happens. Build it again—quickly. Fly it again. Maybe it will fly a little further. Let it crash. See what happens. Build it again quickly . . . " If I were to do it again differently, I would take my own advice, fly the plane, and let it crash. I give permission for my staff to fail and learn all the time. In fact, I encourage it. I need to model that—for myself and for those I lead.

Another thing I would have done differently would be to encourage others to take the reins and facilitate rounds. I have finally started to share the facilitator role with others, but I will admit that my passion for leading instructional rounds made it hard for me to pass it over. In hindsight, I see great benefit in a principal developing her staff's leadership capacity for facilitating rounds early while moving into the role of participating observer.

Lastly, if I could do things differently, I would have pushed myself into sharing this work with a wider audience much sooner. When I looked in the mirror I used to see a leader that thrived within the campus of Monroe Elementary School. I was a compelling and fervent leader—at Monroe. I felt safe and comfortable there. But was I growing? Certainly not to my potential. Thankfully, I was pushed by others to lead outside of the doors of my school. The world today is a world of connectedness and networks. There is amazing potential when we share our work and learn about the work others are having success with. A responsible educator needs to always be developing within themselves and helping others develop too. I have learned to push myself outside my comfort zone—to have a voice and a positive influence in the vast field of education.

Our world is rapidly changing. However, change in education seems to move at a snail's pace and is often faced with resistance on all fronts. Outdated structures and practices are often nostalgically maintained. I believe instructional rounds have a role in moving education forward to a place that prepares our educators to be twenty-first-century professional educators and learners for their students. The process itself is a robust learning experience for teachers that is both personalized and supports systemic change in a school. Instructional rounds are job-embedded, teacher-centered learning experiences rather than external or isolated occurrences in adult learning. Teachers and leaders engage in the same twenty-first-century learning skills of critical thinking, collaboration, communication, and creativity that we need them to plan for in the learning of their students. Instructional rounds allow teachers to see new practices and changes come alive in their own school, making it more comfortable to take a risk and dive into the change. As I shared in the chapters of this book, change is embraced and spread quickly with instructional rounds, and we need to pick up the pace of change in education because we have fallen behind.

Ready for the Future

The futureready.org website, through the Alliance for Excellent Education, lays out frameworks for schools and leadership with a focus on seven key areas. These frameworks help schools consider advancing evidence-based best practices for creating innovative, student-centered, future-ready schools.

The website also includes a Future Ready Principals Framework, and our process of instructional rounds can support two of its directives in particular: "model effective professional learning," and "cultivate a culture of trust."

Instructional rounds are a process and a structure that is timeless. They are a practice that should become regular in a school. The work within that process and structure will grow and change as the educational needs of children (and their teachers) change.

Final Thought

As you consider beginning instructional rounds in your school, I would like to share with you four beliefs from which you can grow your instructional rounds process. First, teacher development thrives in a positive, supportive school culture. Second, instructional rounds set up and promote positivity that will grow your school culture. Third, performance increases when an individual's strengths, rather than their weaknesses, are emphasized. You will leverage greater gains using only strengths. And fourth, self-reflection followed by professional dialogue supports learning and growth. Embed both reflection and dialogue into your process. Honor the interdependence of these last two ideas at all times.

What benefits might come out of having a systematic way for teachers at your school to observe each other teach, have reflective thought about their own teaching as they observe their peers, and collaboratively discuss teaching and learning after their observation?

I invite you to take these four ideas, along with the stories and practices in this book, to create a culture of positive collaboration, school-wide cohesion, and professional learning through instructional rounds.

ACKNOWLEDGMENTS

Mia, Matthew, and Zachary, I am so lucky to be your mom. You are the best gifts I have ever received. I love you. And, Matthew, you are the best writing coach a mom could ask for!

Dave, thank you for supporting my goals and letting me spread my wings while holding me in your heart. I love you.

Syndee Malek, you are my favorite "pusher"! I admire your connectedness, and I can't thank you enough for pushing me to be a connected educator. Your connections opened our doors at Monroe so that we could share our story with others.

Brain Mendler, one day in Detroit you said, "Write a book." Thank you for coaching me to share protocol, strategy, and technique through storytelling. This book would not have been written had it not been for that conversation.

Dave Burgess Consulting team, thank you for taking a risk on me and my story.

To the following friends and family who edited and reviewed my first draft. Thank you for giving your precious time and input before I shared it outside of this circle.

Chris Hensley
Angel Emkow
Carolyn Martin
Tiffany Dean
Melissa Mohlman
Catherine Cost

REFERENCES

City, Elizabeth. "Learning from Instructional Rounds." *Educational Leadership* 69, (October 2011): 36–41.

City, Elizabeth A., Richard F. Elmore, Sarah E. Fiarman, and Lee Teitel. *Instructional Rounds in Education : A Network Approach to Improving Teaching and Learning.* Cambridge, MA: Harvard Education Press, 2014.

Future Ready. "Building Future Ready Leaders." futureready.org.

Hall, Peter A., and Alisa Simeral. *Creating a Culture of Reflective Practice: Capacity-Building for Schoolwide Success.* Alexandria, VA: ASCD, 2017.

Hattie, John. *Visible Learning: A Synthesis of Over 800 Meta-Analyses Relating to Achievement.* New York: Routledge, 2010.

Hearn, Stuart. "Why Managers Should Focus on Employee Strengths to Inspire Great Performance." *Brand Quarterly*, August 2018.

Kachur, Donald, Judith Stout, and Claudia Edwards. *Engaging Teachers in Classroom Walkthroughs.* Cheltenham, VIC: Hawker Brownlow Education, 2014.

Marzano, Robert. "Making the Most of Instructional Rounds—Educational Leadership." *Ascd.Org*, 2011. www.ascd.org/publications/educational-leadership/feb11/vol68/num05/Making-the-Most-of-Instructional-Rounds.aspx.

Marzano, Robert J., Tina Boogren, Tammy Heflebower, Jessica Kanold-McIntyre, and Debra Pickering. *Becoming a Reflective Teacher.* Bloomington, IN: Marzano Research, 2012.

Marzano, Robert, and Michael Toth. "ASCD Express 8.19—Supporting Teacher Growth with Instructional Rounds." *Ascd.Org.*, June 2013. www.ascd.org/ascd-express/vol8/819-marzano.aspx.

Marzano, Robert, Tony Frontier, and David Livingston. *Effective Supervision: Supporting the Art and Science of Teaching.* Moorabbin, VIC: Hawker Brownlow Education, 2011.

Mattos, M., R. DuFour, R. DuFour, R. Eaker, and T. W. Many. (2016). *Learning by Doing: A Handbook for Professional Learning Communities at Work.* Sydney: Solution Tree Australia, 2016.

Mirel, Jeffrey, and Simona Goldin. "Alone in the Classroom: Why Teachers Are Too Isolated." *Atlantic,* April 17, 2012. www.theatlantic.com/national/archive/2012/04/alone-in-the-classroom-why-teachers-are-too-isolated/255976/.

Robinson, Viviane M. J., Claire A. Lloyd, and Kenneth J. Rowe. "The Impact of Leadership on Student Outcomes: An Analysis of the Differential Effects of Leadership Types." *Educational Administration Quarterly* 44, no. 5 (2008): 635–74. https://doi-org /10.1177/0013161x08321509.

Schlechty, Phillip C. "On the Frontier of School Reform with Trailblazers, Pioneers, and Settlers." *Journal of Staff Development* 14, no. 4 (2019): 46–51. eric.ed.gov/?id=EJ482557.

Troen, Vivian, and Katherine Boles. *The Power of Teacher Rounds: A Guide for Facilitators, Principals, & Department Chairs.* Thousand Oaks, CA: Corwin, 2014.

MORE FROM

Dave Burgess Consulting, Inc.

Since 2012, DBCI has been publishing books that inspire and equip educators to be their best. For more information on our titles or to purchase bulk orders for your school, district, or book study, visit **DaveBurgessconsulting.com/DBCIbooks**.

More from the *Lead Like a PIRATE™* Series

Lead Like a PIRATE by Shelley Burgess and Beth Houf
Balance Like a Pirate by Jessica Cabeen, Jessica Johnson, and Sarah Johnson
Lead beyond Your Title by Nili Bartley
Lead with Appreciation by Amber Teamann and Melinda Miller
Lead with Culture by Jay Billy
Lead with Literacy by Mandy Ellis

Like a PIRATE™ Series

Teach Like a PIRATE by Dave Burgess
eXPlore Like a Pirate by Michael Matera
Learn Like a Pirate by Paul Solarz
Play Like a Pirate by Quinn Rollins
Run Like a Pirate by Adam Welcome

Leadership & School Culture

Culturize by Jimmy Casas
Escaping the School Leader's Dunk Tank by Rebecca Coda and Rick Jetter
From Teacher to Leader by Starr Sackstein

The Innovator's Mindset by George Couros
It's OK to Say "They" by Christy Whittlesey
Kids Deserve It! by Todd Nesloney and Adam Welcome
Let Them Speak by Rebecca Coda and Rick Jetter
The Limitless School by Abe Hege and Adam Dovico
The Pepper Effect by Sean Gaillard
The Principled Principal by Jeffrey Zoul and Anthony McConnell
Relentless by Hamish Brewer
The Secret Solution by Todd Whitaker, Sam Miller, and Ryan Donlan
Start. Right. Now. by Todd Whitaker, Jeffrey Zoul, and Jimmy Casas
Stop. Right. Now. by Jimmy Casas and Jeffrey Zoul
They Call Me "Mr. De" by Frank DeAngelis
Unmapped Potential by Julie Hasson and Missy Lennard
Word Shift by Joy Kirr
Your School Rocks by Ryan McLane and Eric Lowe

Technology & Tools

50 Things You Can Do with Google Classroom by Alice Keeler and Libbi Miller
50 Things to Go Further with Google Classroom by Alice Keeler and Libbi Miller
140 Twitter Tips for Educators by Brad Currie, Billy Krakower, and Scott Rocco
Block Breaker by Brian Aspinall
Code Breaker by Brian Aspinall
Google Apps for Littles by Christine Pinto and Alice Keeler
Master the Media by Julie Smith
Reality Bytes by Christine Lion-Bailey, Jesse Lubinsky, Micah Shippee, PhD
Shake Up Learning by Kasey Bell
Social LEADia by Jennifer Casa-Todd
Teaching Math with Google Apps by Alice Keeler and Diana Herrington
Teachingland by Amanda Fox and Mary Ellen Weeks

Teaching Methods & Materials

All 4s and 5s by Andrew Sharos
Boredom Busters by Katie Powell
The Classroom Chef by John Stevens and Matt Vaudrey
The Collaborative Classroom by Trevor Muir
Copyrighteous by Diana Gill
Ditch That Homework by Matt Miller and Alice Keeler
Ditch That Textbook by Matt Miller
Don't Ditch That Tech by Matt Miller, Nate Ridgway, and Angelia Ridgway
EDrenaline Rush by John Meehan
Educated by Design by Michael Cohen, The Tech Rabbi
The EduProtocol Field Guide by Marlena Hebern and Jon Corippo
The EduProtocol Field Guide: Book 2 by Marlena Hebern and Jon Corippo
Instant Relevance by Denis Sheeran
LAUNCH by John Spencer and A.J. Juliani
Make Learning MAGICAL by Tisha Richmond
Pure Genius by Don Wettrick
The Revolution by Darren Ellwein and Derek McCoy
Shift This! by Joy Kirr
Spark Learning by Ramsey Musallam
Sparks in the Dark by Travis Crowder and Todd Nesloney
Table Talk Math by John Stevens
The Wild Card by Hope and Wade King
The Writing on the Classroom Wall by Steve Wyborney

Inspiration, Professional Growth & Personal Development

Be REAL by Tara Martin
Be the One for Kids by Ryan Sheehy
The Coach ADVenture by Amy Illingworth
Creatively Productive by Lisa Johnson
Educational Eye Exam by Alicia Ray

The EduNinja Mindset by Jennifer Burdis
Empower Our Girls by Lynmara Colón and Adam Welcome
Finding Lifelines by Andrew Grieve and Andrew Sharos
The Four O'Clock Faculty by Rich Czyz
How Much Water Do We Have? by Pete and Kris Nunweiler
P Is for Pirate by Dave and Shelley Burgess
A Passion for Kindness by Tamara Letter
The Path to Serendipity by Allyson Apsey
Sanctuaries by Dan Tricarico
The SECRET SAUCE by Rich Czyz
Shattering the Perfect Teacher Myth by Aaron Hogan
Stories from Webb by Todd Nesloney
Talk to Me by Kim Bearden
Teach Better by Chad Ostrowski, Tiffany Ott, Rae Hughart, and Jeff Gargas
Teach Me, Teacher by Jacob Chastain
TeamMakers by Laura Robb and Evan Robb
Through the Lens of Serendipity by Allyson Apsey
The Zen Teacher by Dan Tricarico

Children's Books

Beyond Us by Aaron Polansky
Cannonball In by Tara Martin
Dolphins in Trees by Aaron Polansky
I Want to Be a Lot by Ashley Savage
The Princes of Serendip by Allyson Apsey
The Wild Card Kids by Hope and Wade King
Zom-Be a Design Thinker by Amanda Fox

ABOUT THE AUTHOR

Vicki Wilson has been an educator for over twenty-five years in two districts. She was a classroom teacher for fourteen years before becoming a principal in 2007. Vicki is passionate about education and strives to make it better every day. She is particularly interested in educator learning, leadership, organizational change, progressive and innovative practices in education, and leveraging best practices in her school to make improvements so that all students get the best possible education. As the proud principal of Monroe Elementary School in Wyandotte, Michigan, she enjoys watching children learn under the challenge, guidance, and support of the passionate and dedicated educators in her school. Monroe is a learning and student-centered school that values both student and adult collaborative learning. Under Vicki's leadership, Monroe Elementary was named a nationally recognized Model PLC School by Solution Tree in 2018.

Vicki believes in finding that sweet spot of presenting challenge and providing support for her staff and for herself. Believing in risk-taking and the value of learning from mistakes, Vicki often tells her staff, "Just fly the plane and see what happens. If it crashes, that's okay. Learn from it, rebuild it quickly, and launch it again." This is a mindset she encourages staff to model with their students as well.

Vicki is honored to serve on the regional board of MEMSPA (Michigan Elementary and Middle School Principals Association), where she discovered the benefit of connecting and networking with other educational leaders to make a difference beyond the walls of one school by having an impact and voice in the field of education—the most important work in the world today. She enjoys connecting with a professional learning network (PLN) through Twitter, Twitter chats, blogs, and at events. Vicki is an author, blogger, and presenter.

Married to David, she has three beautiful and kind children—a daughter, Mia, and twin boys, Matthew and Zachary.

Made in the USA
Las Vegas, NV
07 February 2024